"In her book *Own Best Friend*, Dr. Kristina Hallett delivers a message that is dear to my heart. I am a fibromyalgia patient, and self-care has been the key that has unlocked a life I love to live and my future. Unfortunately, many of the clients and students I work with don't know how to translate the concept of self-care into reality. They often think it means getting a massage or taking a bubble bath or meditating. It can include those things, to be sure. Ultimately, however, self-care is about treating yourself the way you'd treat someone you love. It's about being your own best friend. Dr. Hallett's EMPOWERS process provides a practical, step-by-step framework for cultivating a relationship with yourself that goes beyond massages and bubble baths to provide something deeper and more lasting: a loving and nurturing relationship with yourself."

Tami Stackelhouse, Founder, International Fibromyalgia
Coaching Institute, IFCInstitute.com

"I have always believed that we are the CEOs of our own destinies. In her book *Own Best Friend* Kristina Hallett takes this notion to a much deeper spiritual level. She provides a guide to help us live more fully by believing in ourselves and the powers within us."

Carol A. Leary, PhD, President, Bay Path University,
Author of *Achieving the Dream*

Own Best Friend

Eight Steps to a Life of Purpose, Passion, and Ease

KRISTINA HALLETT PhD, ABPP

NEW YORK

NASHVILLE • MELBOURNE • VANCOUVER

Own Best Friend
Eight Steps to a Life of Purpose, Passion, and Ease

Published in New York, New York, by Morgan James Publishing in partnership with Difference Press. Morgan James is a trademark of Morgan James, LLC. www.MorganJamesPublishing.com

The Morgan James Speakers Group can bring authors to your live event. For more information or to book an event visit The Morgan James Speakers Group at www.TheMorganJamesSpeakersGroup.com.

ISBN 978-1-68350-629-4 paperback
ISBN 978-1-68350-630-0 eBook
Library of Congress Control Number: 2017909502

Cover Design by:
Rachel Lopez
www.r2cdesign.com

Interior Design by:
Bonnie Bushman
The Whole Caboodle Graphic Design

In an effort to support local communities, raise awareness and funds, Morgan James Publishing donates a percentage of all book sales for the life of each book to Habitat for Humanity Peninsula and Greater Williamsburg.

Get involved today! Visit
www.MorganJamesBuilds.com

Dedication

For Sandra.
From the first, you have been my light, my love,
my inspiration, my precious daughter. This one's for you.

Table of Contents

Foreword

In *Own Best Friend* Dr. Kristina Hallett takes on simple themes that have gotten lost in the swamp of modern life—living with meaning, passion, and purpose, and basically being our own personal spirit guides. We can access GPS satellites to guide us in nearly every corner of the planet, but we have lost our own personal guidance systems—and too many people report feeling lost and alone, even when interconnectivity and the illusion of connection is ubiquitous. Ads for antidepressants pepper the landscape of self-help daytime television. Something is not quite right.

Shortly before I spoke with Kristina about her book, I had the privilege of completing an immersive pilgrimage to temples in South India. The process evoked spirituality, mindfulness, and patience. Lots of patience. The temples are treasure troves of sculpture, ancient architecture, jewels, flowers, and a sensory tsunami—smell, sight, sounds, touch, and taste.

As I stood in a queue that proceeded to the inner sanctum of the temple to witness the "featured" deity, I saw many other small statuary in nooks set along the way. The statues reflected myths that carried themes of duty, obedience, discipline, sacrifice, fate, and hope—heavy mantles to shoulder.

The myth of Ganesh is a favorite standard in the repository of Hindu mythology, and one that has been embraced by the West. To make a long myth short, Ganesh was the son of Shiva and Parvati, and his head was replaced by the head of an elephant, due to a bit of a misunderstanding. He is a benevolent spirit revered as a remover of obstacles, patron of the arts, and the overseer of new beginnings. It is his standing as a remover of obstacles that has held the most resonance for the West, and a statue of Ganesh often serves as a talisman for difficult situations.

At one of the temples I visited, I looked at a particular Ganesh statue and had a moment of clarity in which I recognized that perhaps nearly all obstacles are perceptual and illusory. The temptation is to turn to Ganesh to grease the way to personal goals (relationships, education, career, money)—but what about the obstacles we set within ourselves that block us ("I can't do this" "No one starts a new career this late" "I'm not enough" "What if they say no?")? Even the practical obstacles— money, time, other people—are, in fact, internal constructions.

So, does that mean that simply thinking differently about a situation would remove the obstacle? This is the central premise of cognitive behavioral therapy. People pray to Ganesh to remove what are believed to be literal barriers, but perhaps we all have an inner divinity that could allow us to think differently about these obstacles and re-render them.

The neuroscientist Robert Sapolsky makes the argument that zebras don't get ulcers, because they do not worry about small things—they only expend their sympathetic nervous systems on the real dangers, like a charging lion. The amount of time and mental bandwidth we humans expend on the *what ifs*, *shoulds*, and *supposed tos* results in significant wear and tear on our minds, bodies, and souls.

What are these barriers, obstacles, fears, and anxieties? While many are real—money, illness, deadlines—most are created. Even with the real barriers, what tends to be distorted is the narrative we create around them ("If I don't make this deadline, my life will be ruined" "If I don't make enough money, I'm not a success"). Many of these barriers are created from the expectations others have for us to get the "right" career, the "right" partner, the "right" life. The risk then becomes that life is about living the narratives of others, rather than our own narratives. We become players in someone else's script, rather than crafting our own. Perhaps ancient mythologies offered through Hindu deities and modern neuroscience all converge on a similar riff—that we waste time on fears that are illusory.

More important may be the idea that we want to move past the barriers that block us, that keep us from living fully and authentically, that can often become both an excuse for pushing past our fears and a prison that keeps us from living in alignment with our true selves. In that singular hope of moving past those barriers, we make pleas to elephant-headed gods or wish on shooting stars, instead of recognizing that we have the power to remove these obstacles ourselves.

Anaïs Nin writes, "It takes courage to push yourself to places that you have never been before... to test your limits... to break through barriers. And the day came when the risk it took to remain tight inside the bud was more painful than the risk it took to blossom." *Own Best Friend* is a handbook of sorts—a guide to breaking through your own barriers to take the risk to blossom.

When we live in accordance with the expectations of others, we are often hampered in our decision-making—whether the topic is the prosaic stuff of life ("Where should we eat dinner?") or the big ticket issues ("Should I marry him?"). We become confused by the warring voices—society, family, self. While the scaffolds of other people's narratives can serve as an exoskeleton of sorts, they also limit us and can leave us feeling sapped. Living the lives of others is a way of eschewing the anxiety of responsibility—and so we lapse into the easy defense of projecting our regrets, losses, and missed lives on others.

The principles of Dr. Hallett's book are about becoming acquainted with and trusting the one person who will always have your back—you. She acknowledges that this is not an easy journey, and that to live passionately and purposefully means taking a journey inward to become acquainted with your own power, resources, and courage. She offers daily practices to reconnect you to your best self and to help you practice being that best self. The ideas that we don't deserve to be happy, don't have the time to live fully, don't have the courage to "go for it" are tethers that keep us tied to the ground, and Dr. Hallett teaches us how to cut those tethers, one by one.

The journey you will take within these pages is no different from the journey of authenticity that is the core principle of all myths—*The Ramayana*, *The Iliad*, *The Odyssey*, *The Lord of the Rings*, and even *The Wizard of Oz* (the search for courage, wisdom, love, and belongingness). As echoed by psychological theorists like Freud, Maslow, Murray, and Rogers, and the epic poets of yore, we know what we need, but we need a little guidance to get there. The spirit guide for such a journey of authenticity can be an ancient mystic, Frodo, Dorothy, or, in this case, Dr. Kristina Hallett.

Dr. Ramani Durvasula
Los Angeles, California

Chapter 1

Introduction: Getting to Your Best Life

"I ain't settlin' for anything less than everything."
Sugarland, "Settlin"

How are things going in your life? Really. Are you living your best life? I want you to have everything you want—starting now. I know how easy it is to get caught up in the million things you have to do, and to end up feeling tired, stressed, overwhelmed, and as if you are missing out. Missing out on feeling happy, on living with ease, on being who you want to be, and on living with purpose and passion. This book offers simple solutions in all of those areas (and more).

How do you know if this book is for you? Well, have you ever had any of these thoughts?

- *I'm missing out on my life.*
- *Time is passing. I'm just not happy, and it's interfering with my relationships, with my children, and with my job.*
- *I'm stressed, and it's only getting worse.*
- *I keep trying different things, but nothing works. I'm tired, and I feel like there must be more to life than this.*
- *I don't know if I will ever really be happy. Every time I feel like I've got it together, something happens and I'm right back where I started.*
- *Sleep? Who can possibly sleep when there's so much to do? Exercise? Time for myself? Sure, like I could fit that in with everything else that has to get done.*

If you have had *any* of those thoughts—I hear you. Life is so busy, and there's never enough time to get it all done. Or at least that's how it seems to you (and probably to lots of your friends). You finally manage to fit a "girl's night" into your busy schedule and, before you know it, you're talking with each other about the kids and how it's running you ragged to cart them all over town to all their activities (but you *want* them to do all that stuff, so should you really complain?). The conversation shifts to work and, as much as you love your job, is that really all there is to pump you up so you feel good? And relationships—whether or not you're in one—are complicated (that's the funniest Facebook status ever; is *any* relationship not complicated?).

I know a few women who have been in the same place you are. Women who sometimes sat in their cars for "just a few minutes" after arriving home, in order to catch their breath before jumping into the endless lists of things that absolutely *must* be done. Women who thought about hiding out in the bathroom to get a moment of peace (and did that). Women who juggled a dozen decisions and responsibilities before having breakfast. Women who wanted to *have it all*—and who wondered more times than they could count if that was even remotely possible for anyone.

These women are awesome friends, mothers, daughters, spouses, girlfriends, bosses, and co-workers. You know these women. They are *your* friends. Your sisters, cousins, mothers, daughters, and co-workers. When you meet them, you are so impressed by who they are. You see how hard they work, how many things they do, *how much they care.* You look at them and you wonder, *How do they do it? How do they juggle home, job, and a relationship? How do they always seem to have an encouraging word or smile? How is it that they seem to manage, and more than that, manage* happily? *What's their secret? Why don't I know it? And how do I get it?*

These are women who have had many of the same doubts, concerns, struggles, and challenges you're having. The actual circumstances they have faced may look different, but inside, where it really counts, they *get* you because they have been in the same exact place as you. The super fabulous amazing news is that *you* can have what they now have. You can live a life that's rewarding and fulfilling. You can have a job you love, and time to yourself, and *still* get everything done. You can feel good about who you are. You can have a sense of inner purpose and live the life you want. You can be happy—*really* happy.

→→→ -←←←

If you met Theresa, you would truly think she has it all. She has a fabulous job she absolutely loves and that allows her to continue to grow and develop. She has strong friendships and some wonderful family relationships (okay, nothing is ever really perfect; she has some issues with her mother, but, hey, it's not getting her down and, overall, it's a lot better than it used to be). Theresa is married and has three wonderful, active, involved children. If she walked into the room, you'd be impressed with her poise and the way she carries herself. *This* is someone who feels good about who she is. You wouldn't be surprised to find out that she's recently decided to further her education and is taking on *one more thing*, in addition to the gazillion things she already does with such grace and ease—because you could tell she could somehow handle it all. On top of all of that, she goes to the gym on a regular basis and has gotten the hang of that "mindfulness" thing you hear about all the time. But this wasn't always her story.

When I began working with Theresa, many of those characteristics were true—on the outside. She had a job that she liked (not the one she has now). She had a nice house. She had kids and was married, and had what seemed like a good relationship. But what you might have seen on the outside wasn't at all reflected on the inside. Theresa was *stressed*. She really struggled with her boss, and that impacted her satisfaction with her job. She was always rushing from one responsibility to another and hadn't seen the inside of a gym in a long time. She had friends but didn't feel really connected to them—because there was no time to nurture those relationships. And there was certainly no time for *herself*. Ha. That was not even on the never-ending list of things to do.

Theresa would find herself agreeing to help out, taking on more and more. At night, she had trouble stopping her thoughts from circling around and around, and she felt like there *had* to be a better way. She had a vague sense of wanting "more" in her life but knew that wasn't going to happen, even if she figured out what the "more" was, because there was no time, she was too tired, and there was too much going on to even think about it. At various points, she tried to read self-help books people had recommended, but nothing seemed to work (and, seriously, if one more person suggested she simply "make time" for herself, she thought she would scream). She was "sorta" happy, trying to keep a positive attitude but feeling like she was slowly sinking, with no end in sight. She knew something had to change, quickly, but she was at a loss to figure out what and how.

This book will show you what Theresa discovered through our work together, including the tips, tricks, and hacks she used to get to where she is now. Theresa is at a place where her inside and her outside match. She really *is* happy and fulfilled. That doesn't mean she never has crappy days or never gets frustrated. But by using this system, life doesn't get her down. In fact, life looks pretty damn good to Theresa. She has gotten a much better job, getting higher pay doing work she loves and that challenges her, and she has a great boss. She has a close circle of friends she sees regularly, both with and without her kids and husband. She's excited to finally be acting on her long-held, secret dream of pursuing an advanced degree. She's eating and sleeping well, and she's healthy. Theresa has started to do yoga and feels a sense of inner peace and contentment she hadn't known was possible. This book will show you how you can get that, too.

>>> <<<

Or maybe you're more like Bethany. Bethany described her life this way when we first met: "I need help. I know my life *looks* good. I love my job, I have a great boyfriend, and my family is really supportive and wonderful. But I'm anxious all the time—except at work—and I can't seem to do the things I know I *should* do, like exercise, eat right, that kind of stuff. I feel really stuck. *I'm just not happy, and I don't know how to fix it.* If I could figure out how to get motivated, I could do those things. Then I would lose weight, have time for friends, and I'm sure I would feel better. But right now, I can't seem to stick to anything. I've gone to therapy—a lot. It would help for a while and then everything would slip away, and I'd be back where I started. I'm so sick of this. I want to enjoy my life, not keep repeating the same pattern. And you know what else?

When my boyfriend says he thinks I'm beautiful, or that he's proud of me, I want to actually *believe* him, instead of thinking, *You're just saying that to try and make me feel better.* I can't ever take a compliment from anyone, even my family. They're always giving me a hard time about that, saying I should see myself the way they do. If only what they said was true, I would. But honestly, I don't get it. I know who I am, and it's not who I want to be."

Bethany was really struggling. She could see she had a lot going for her, and she appreciated it, but it didn't seem to matter. She was in quicksand, and the more she tried to get out, the deeper she sank. She was looking for answers and solutions that would *truly make a difference in her life.* She was sick of moving one step forward and two steps back. And she was absolutely sick of feeling that she *should* be happy when she wasn't.

Like Theresa, Bethany was willing to really *work* at understanding and applying the strategies that you will read about in this book. After doing that for eight weeks, Bethany said, "Wow. I didn't ever think I would say this, but I'm good. Really good. I've been practicing everything we talked about and it's working. I went to a yoga class with my mom a few days ago, and I actually had fun. I still can't do half the poses, but I'm not worrying about it, or worrying about how I look doing it. And guess what? Yesterday someone at work gave me a compliment and I said, 'Thank you.' And I meant it. I suddenly realized the voice in my head that used to say, *Uh-huh, sure* wasn't there anymore. I was so excited. And this time, *I feel like I get it.* I can tell my old patterns have finally shifted."

>>>- -<<<

There's one more woman I want you to meet—Sandi. I used to (lovingly) think of her as "the self-help guru." She was always listening to podcasts, reading books, and checking out different programs in search of a way to "get herself back". When I met her, she told me she "used to feel happy and fulfilled." Then life got in the way, and she couldn't seem to find her mojo. She loved authors like Tara Brach, Pema Chodron, Brené Brown (so do I), but all those wise words weren't working. She *knew* all the "right" things to do, but they weren't enough.

When Sandi couldn't sleep at night, she'd get up and start googling (that's how she started finding all those self-help guides). She would look up anything she thought might solve her problem, including: *stress, happiness, self-esteem, inner purpose, find what's missing in your life, tired all the time,* and *meditation.* Usually that led to one of two things: either she would find a new approach to start trying, or she would feel even more discouraged, which made everything worse. Sandi's issue was frustrating because often she would see a brief improvement, and then something would happen (usually at work), and she'd be right back at square one. She was full of self-doubt, angry that she couldn't "get it right," and yearning for what felt like an impossible dream.

Sandi wanted to figure out a way to manage her schedule so that she had some time for herself. She wanted to know a way to spend more quality time with her daughters and to be more connected with her husband (instead of feeling like he was her third child). She wanted to get back into the activities she used to love, like hiking. And she wanted to not feel so defensive or left out when her boss didn't include her in a meeting or a conversation. Most of all, she wanted to find her inner purpose and live a happy, meaningful life.

Since Sandi was already familiar with lots of great resources (she's shared some amazing books with me), at first we both thought that would give her a leg up on learning and implementing the program in this book. We were both right and wrong. Some of what I taught Sandi was familiar to her and, even though that let her go deeper in some areas, it also got in the way. Since Sandi sometimes thought she already knew what she (thought she) needed to do, sometimes she didn't really pay attention when we discussed it. Luckily, we picked up on the problem quickly and adjusted. Sandi figured out that when she was so focused on searching, she wasn't fully in the moment. We put that, and other puzzle pieces together, to show a different picture of her life than what she'd seen before.

Sandi's life has really changed. She got a big promotion at work, takes weekends off (she's a reformed workaholic), has been able to participate in activities at her daughters' schools, and she's no longer googling at two a.m. She has also found her inner purpose, which was not at all what she'd thought it would be. She's taking more risks, and she's happy.

Sandi told me she didn't get her old self back; instead, she's a new, improved version of herself. She still has lots of potential stressors in her life, but she handles life in a whole new way. She's not perfect—no one is—but she feels grounded, confident, and clear about who she is and where she's going. Sandi followed the system in this book and has never looked back.

⋙ ⋘

Do the stories of these women ring any bells for you? Are there parts of Theresa's, Bethany's, or Sandi's lives and words that are similar to what you've been going through, or that are like what you want to find? If you follow this process, you will achieve *your* version of success. Even though there are commonalities, it's your situation that matters to you. The great news is that *this process will work for you and your situation.*

In order to make the most of these strategies, we need to cover some basic ground first. This may not be the first time you're hearing some of this. That's okay. Hang in there, and let yourself really pay attention. To have the life you've always wanted, you have to let the pieces come together in a new way instead of anticipating the outcome.

Let's get started.

Stress—What It's Really for and Why It's Good

What happens when you feel stressed? Your muscles tense up, your head hurts, your stomach hurts, you eat more (or way less), you have trouble sleeping (or sleep too much), you get irritable, cranky, less patient, less tolerant, feel anxious, feel depressed, and—to top it all off—you're likely to get sick. As if all the rest wasn't bad enough, adding a cold or some other kind of bug into the mix is just *too much*.

Stress isn't all bad (honest). Stress is what gets your fight or flight mechanism revved up and going. Back in the prehistoric days, this was literally a lifesaver. There you were, taking a nice walk in the woods, looking around for something good to eat, and then *BAM*. Huge saber-toothed tiger barreling down the path toward you, figuring you'd be a tasty before-dinner snack. The stress mechanism snaps into place, hormones flood your body and brain, your heartbeat speeds up (you don't want to *be* dinner, you want to *find* dinner), and you take off running like a bat out of hell, hightailing it back to your safe, warm cave. In that circumstance, stress gives you super-human speed and dexterity, and you manage to avoid being steak tartare.

Of course, once you're back in the cave and the tiger has gone on to find more accessible prey, you're likely to collapse. All those superpowers are gone and you're pretty much a washed- out wreck, trying to stop replaying the memory over and over again. The adrenaline that flooded your body has left, and you're remembering why being a vegetarian is the new plan of action. If you ever leave the cave again, that is.

That's the cycle of stress and the way it works to help you take care of an immediate, urgent need. You've experienced the same thing in lots of different situations. Remember that time you were driving down the highway to work, going a safe five miles per hour over the speed limit and singing out loud to the radio? No one was around to hear you, it was a beautiful day, one of your favorite songs was playing, and you were rocking it out. Suddenly, *BAM*, a car cut in front of you from the right, at the exact second the car ahead of you slammed on it's brakes. In the blink of an eye, you knew what was going to happen: a major three-car pile-up and a really good chance that you were going to be hurt badly (never mind the damage to your beautiful car, and being late to work). You slammed on the brakes, glanced to the left, swerved into the empty lane there, and managed to avoid a horrible collision, all the while noticing every single little detail about the situation. It seemed to happen in slow motion—and you're *still* not sure how you managed to not only live through that one, but keep on driving afterward.

A few minutes later, as you were pulling off the highway, you noticed that you were shaking and still trying to catch your breath. You were barely going the speed limit by then, and you were leaving at least four car lengths between yourself and the car in front of you. When you got to work, your breathing had returned to normal. You had decided to get a coffee from Starbucks at lunch instead of on the way to work, since getting stationary and out of the car was suddenly a bigger priority. After sharing the story of your near-miss and the jerk who almost ended it all, you felt like you'd already worked a whole day.

The parallels between that death-defying tiger incident and the bad driver incident are pretty clear. Both times your body automatically responded with what was needed to save the day, and then it needed a break to even itself out again. This is how stress works in your favor, by helping you handle an emergency situation. That stress reaction occurs whenever your body or brain senses a threat and provides you with the ability to act. The situation doesn't have to be as dramatic as the examples above, either. You know that sinking internal feeling you get before you stand up in front of an audience to give a presentation (even if it's only to announce who's heading the Girl Scout cookie drive this year)? That's also a stress reaction. Your body and mind are preparing you to face a threat, getting you ready to stand up or run away.

"Stress is caused by being 'here' but wanting to be 'there.'"
Eckhart Tolle

That Eckhart Tolle quote is a good description of what we've been talking about, and also describes a different kind of stress. The "I have too much to do in too little time" kind of stress. If you think about the last time you really felt overwhelmed and "stressed," you'll probably realize that you experienced most of the sensations mentioned above. Your brain felt overcrowded, maybe like a headache was coming on, you were jittery (and not from too much coffee.), you couldn't seem to think straight, and the list of things you had to finish was longer than Santa's Christmas list for the entire world. Chances are, you were not your most pleasant, happiest self in that moment. All those feelings that were flooding through your body are the same responses to stress, but they were applied to a situation that *seemed* like life-or-death, but probably really wasn't. That doesn't really matter to your body though— once those stress hormones break through the starting gate, nothing is stopping them without a major intervention—and not just "take a breath and calm down" (how many people do you think that actually works for?).

The truth is that you really *aren't* able to talk yourself into calming down in that moment. Those pesky little stress hormones are too busy responding to the orders of the amygdala in your mid-brain. That's the place in your brain that sets off the internal fire alarm, the "Go, go, GO!" reaction to the perceived danger. Only, *oops*. The amygdala is so busy sounding the alarm that it's not letting your thinking brain (your pre-frontal cortex) assess the situation and determine how big the immediate danger really is. As far as the amygdala is concerned, your endless list of things to do is the same as a drooling, growling saber-toothed tiger (or the thoughtless driver who is going to cause your imminent death). Since your amygdala is determined to help you save yourself from this horrible threat, it ramps the internal siren and lights louder and louder. *Of course* you can't think in that circumstance, and your head hurts, just like if you were really standing in front of a blaring alarm with flashing lights. In real life, fire alarms are meant to be piercing to get your attention so you will *get out*. Your amygdala is doing the same thing inside your head. It has one job, and that's to save you from danger. So once the emergency switch is tripped, the alarm is going to continue to go off (and get louder and louder) until the danger is gone.

The way to stop the madness is to re-set the alarm. Sounds like it should be simple, right? But if you can't think clearly, remembering where the switch is to turn it off can be a challenge. A big one. That's when you need to have some built-in systems to help you out—a way to notice the earliest signs of impending "danger" *before* the alarms are blaring and you're in full fight-or-flight mode. There's another mode that can happen then, that's the freeze mode. Have you ever seen a rabbit hopping along across your lawn? You see it out of the corner of your eye and turn, yelling, "Look at the bunny!" (Hey, bunnies are cute. It's only natural to point it out.) What does the bunny do when you start yelling? It freezes. It stops right in its tracks and is so still you might not even be able to see it. At least, that's what the bunny is hoping. Its first instinct is to stop all movement and pretend it's invisible. *Nope, no bunny. Not here. Just go about your business, you big scary monster. You can't see me.*

We do the same thing sometimes. It's an instinct, part of the flight-fight-freeze pattern. If the danger doesn't see you, it might pass on by, leaving you alone. You've probably seen a deer do the same thing. The freeze response is hard-wired into our brains, right along with the instinct to fight or to run. For some reason, the freeze reaction doesn't get talked about as much, but it really should. "Frozen in fear" is a standard reaction in scary movies (right before the screaming and the running *toward* the homicidal maniac, but that part is just Hollywood. You know that *you* wouldn't be the one running toward the guy with the ax—because every time that happens in a movie you think to yourself, "Go! Get out of there. Do *not* go into the cellar!"). I bet you've seen (maybe even been) the child who stops in her tracks with her hands behind her back when asked, "What are you doing? What's in your hands?" *Stop. Freeze.* "Who me? Nothing,"—hoping the cookies (or the mom) will magically disappear.

Instinct. It's powerful. And it needs a powerful push to change the automatic course that it sets into motion.

In this book, I'll share with you ways that stress can become your friend (but not an overpowering, clingy kind of friend). You will have the opportunity to dive deep into eight powerful steps that will open the doors to lasting change, increasing your resilience, productivity, happiness, and freedom. You will uncover some of your hidden challenges and move forward from your stuck places. I know this system works, both from the successes of so many clients, and from my own experience. In the next chapter, I'll share how I came to these discoveries.

Chapter 2
My Love Letter to You

"If an egg is broken by an outside force, life ends.
If broken by an inside force, life begins."
Jim Kwik

This is a book for you, but it started with my own process. I had a professional reason for developing this process, but also a highly personal reason.

I've been working as a clinical psychologist for the last 23 years (wow, I hadn't realized how long it was until I actually wrote that). I have a couple of specialty areas, but one of them (the one closest to my heart) is working with women who are going through life changes. This means the entire gamut of changes—from first apartment and first real job, to having a first child (or second, or twins—you get the idea), to struggling with identifying life goals, to managing a vocation and a family, to getting a divorce or starting a long-term relationship, to dealing with the questions of *Who am I and what am I* supposed *to be doing in my life?* to the huge question of *Is this all there is?*

The women I've worked with have come from many walks of life and have had equally varied sets of life experiences. To say they have been a diverse bunch is to really understate the degree of difference among them. And yet, over the years, as I worked with women (teenagers, 20-somethings, new moms, career-focused and family-focused, "middle-aged" (I hate that term.), single, never married, married, divorced, widowed, remarried, lesbian, straight, questioning), I began to notice similarities. Really striking similarities. I started to pay (closer) attention and discovered that I talked about the same general eight areas with everyone. Not always in the same order, but it was rare for at least one of the eight not to be a part of the conversation. Even when I was convinced that a certain woman was dealing with an entirely unique situation, all of the eight areas would eventually be important topics of discussion.

Once I caught on to that trend (honestly, it took a while, because I initially saw the differences in the women's circumstances more than the repetition of themes), it seemed really clear. In fact, I wondered how it was possible that I had *not* noticed sooner how closely the core issues were *in every situation.* You would think that after only a few years of this work I might have noticed that I was talking about the same kind of things with client after client after client. Becoming aware of it took a while.

Which leads me to the personal reason for developing this process.

I'm a woman (you can probably tell that from my name). The reason this is important is that *I was not exempt from needing to learn all the same lessons as the women I worked with were addressing.*

A clinical psychologist spends a lot of years learning about human behavior, emotions, and ways to support people through their own growth processes. A recommended part of this learning typically involves going through your own therapeutic growth. I did that—I went to therapy, worked to improve my self-care, and learned to be "assertive" and speak up about my feelings, opinions, needs, and wants. I read a lot of self-help books (why reinvent the wheel, right?) and talked with friends and colleagues about the challenges I faced. If you had asked me back then, I would have told you that I knew myself really well. I understood the perspectives I had developed while growing up. I knew how to apply a theoretically based understanding to my particular circumstances, and could easily list the "issues" I had faced and overcome. I could differentiate between my inner feelings, the feelings projected by the women I worked with, and the countertransferential feelings that got triggered when I heard or experienced specific stories or interactions. (*Countertransference* is what happens when someone is talking about something and you have an internal reaction to what is going on that's based on your own history, rather than on an empathic response to what they are sharing).

So, with all of that knowledge, time, and personal work invested, I should have had it all together, right? Ha. In many ways, I did. I did work that I was passionate about, that continually intrigued me, and that kept my interest. I had an amazing daughter and awesome people in my life. I had family who cared for me, and friends who were as close as family. I had education, shelter, clothing, food, and general good health. I even had dogs. What more could I possibly have wanted?

Of course, there was another side. My first marriage ended early on. After that, I was living as a single, working mother and I usually collapsed into bed much later than my self-help books recommended, as I tried to manage the household, caring for my young daughter, and all the other things that life throws at us on a daily basis. Lying in bed at night, waiting for the blessed relief of sleep, I would wonder what I was doing wrong. Why, despite having the outward trappings of a successful life, did I feel like I was missing the boat? Why couldn't I seem to find the "right" relationship? Why did juggling all the pieces mean there was never any room for me? Why did I feel so guilty if I took time for myself, and feel resentful when I wasn't able to? Why did I wish for someone to help me, but never managed to ask for help, because I believed I "should" be able to handle things on my own? Why did the day only have 24 hours instead of at least 30? And why couldn't I seem to function on less than six hours of sleep. Six hours would have come in handy. In a few extra hours per day, I could vacuum, pick up the house, do laundry, and maybe even exercise.

Most of all, I wondered why I was not happier. In my early life, my list of what would make me happy was pretty simple. I wanted a well-paying job in my field of choice; children; a home (with dogs); friends; and a happy, loving relationship. I had four out of those five, and I wasn't really happy. Even when I *was* in a good, loving relationship, I wasn't as happy as I wanted to be. I knew it wasn't about the relationship. I had finally figured out the relationship issue was a plus if it worked, but it wasn't necessary to my happiness. I had the individual components of what would make me happy, but something was still missing.

Initially, I decided that time was the missing link. If I could be more efficient, plan my life a little better, then it would all fall into place. I worked on that, but nope. Some things got better, others didn't. I appreciated the amount of things I could accomplish, but it didn't really impact the happy factor. It started my life-long love of planners, datebooks, and all things office-supply-related, but it didn't get me the results I wanted.

The next issue up for consideration was energy. I was tired. Bone-deep, soul-wrenching tired. Since I had already decided that my lack of happiness wasn't fully about the time factor (I mean, everyone is less tired when they sleep more; that's obvious), I figured that maybe increasing my overall energy level would result in feeling better (and being happier). One major obstacle I hadn't solved was *how* to increase energy in the face of limited time. I knew that if I was able to exercise I would feel less tired and more energetic. It was a circular argument, and it all came back to not having enough hours in the day.

And so it went. I regularly reviewed all the areas of my life to try and figure out the secret to feeling better and enjoying my life. I wanted to be happy, feel fulfilled, love my job, spend quality time with my daughter… *and* have a clean house and pay my bills. *I wanted it all.* When I saw other women at the grocery store, at work, at the library, it seemed that many of them had conquered what was still such a stuck point in my life. I was simultaneously working with women who were dealing with variations on the same themes I was struggling with in my life, but whatever gems of genius I stumbled upon for them didn't cut it in my own life. Applying my own advice? *Check.* Awesome, fast results? *Nope.*

And then one day it hit me. I was in the shower, running through what I had to get done over the course of the day (doesn't everyone have vital revelations in the shower?), and a little spark of something began to glimmer in the back of my mind. When I put words to it, it was this: *The* sum total *of the areas I worked with women to address was greater than the individual components.* That was one of those pseudo-math moments that distracted me, as I tried to figure out how two plus two equaled more than four. Giving up on the numerical intricacies, I focused on the idea of *cumulative change.* It wasn't so much the specific, individual changes that resulted in making the difference—*it was getting the whole package together.*

As I thought about who of my clients had made changes and reached the seemingly elusive states of "happiness" and "personal fulfillment," and who had finished their work and truly "had it all," it became obvious that those were the women who approached their life as *a whole*, rather than as the sum of a bunch of different parts.

Those women had mastered the art of perspective and applied it to everything they did. They were the women who were confident in themselves and who glowed with a sense of inner purpose. They were the women who had found their true selves, gotten into their groove, and who *lived it*.

When I'd met those women, every one of them, they had been in a place of disarray, discontent, and discouragement. Because we worked closely together, I knew the trials and tribulations they had faced— the disappointments, "failures," and often some version of tragic loss. Along the way to dealing with each of those challenges, for each of those women, something had clicked. The time it took them to change wasn't always the same (although I later discovered it was actually pretty close if the real determining factor, which was how sick and tired they were of being sick and tired, and how badly they wanted things to be different in their lives was taken into consideration). When a woman came in to see me who was really *ready to transform*, the changes happened quickly. It suddenly hit me like a freight train: The women who were successful in getting and living the lives they wanted—lives of meaning, purpose, and happiness—had decided to *stop living small*.

By the time of that amazing shower insight, I had made some serious changes myself. I'd always been a fairly positive person, but by that point, I had learned a lot of specific techniques (based in the science of Positive Psychology), with amazing results, and was using those techniques with great success in my own life. Overall, I was doing better emotionally; I was more active (my daughter was also older, which helped); I was in a healthy, committed relationship, and I had a better job that was constantly challenging me to learn and grow. I had started to do yoga, and for the first time I was able to personally experience a meditative state. (I have one of those minds that is always, and I mean *always*, active. Practicing yoga, I was finally able to fully let go and "be." It was amazing. If you haven't tried yoga, I strongly suggest that you do.)

I got so much out of doing yoga that I decided to take the yoga teacher training course, so I could teach yoga to clients I worked with at a community mental health center. Those clients didn't have the access to yoga, for reasons of finances, transportation, or physical limitations. Wanting to share the wonderful gift of yoga with them motivated me to do the teacher training, even though I was scared out of my mind. I can't really explain *why* I was so uncomfortable, I just knew I was.

The yoga teacher training involved a lot of focus on personal awareness and development, in addition to learning specific yoga poses and the formatting of running a class. It was right up my alley, given that I'd already done years of self-work. All was going smoothly until, one day, my teacher asked me why I was "so committed to living small." I remember looking at her and saying something like, "I don't live small. I've pursued all of my dreams and interests. I'm not living small." I proceeded to give her a list of *blah, blah, blah*—all the risks, triumphs, and changes I had gone through over the previous decade or so.

Inside myself, something different was going on. I was simultaneously furious that she would describe me that way—"living small"—and confused as to what she was talking about. So I did what any good right-brained person does, and tried to "figure it out." I talked to friends, family, anyone I could engage in the conversation of what it means to "live small." I thought about it and considered dozens of hypotheses (many of which centered around my teacher being entirely incorrect in her assessment). After a while, I stopped actively thinking about it, since I hadn't come to any kind of resolution, but that annoyed me, too. The phrase continued to pop up now and then, but I never got any further in deciphering the meaning of it or its application to my life. I continued on with the work I was doing. Life got better and better. I was mostly happy, most of the time. I was generally fulfilled. I was practicing all the things I taught to others, and it was working for them and for me. If there were still occasions when I felt like something was missing, or felt like there should be something more, well—I wasn't expecting life to be perfect, and so I didn't really have much to complain about.

Back to what happened after I had my big "aha" moment in the shower. I could feel the weight of the truth of that realization. Something deep within me responded to it, opened up, and it clicked. It wasn't only about the women I worked with, who successfully got it all together. *It applied to me, too.* That was what my teacher was talking about when she asked me about living small. It was about *me.* "Living small" was like looking in a mirror and not recognizing the person reflected back at you.

The answer to *actually* having a life of meaning, happiness, and purpose, of fully living and being able to "have it all" meant using the multitude of tips, techniques, and knowledge I had been sharing (and using), *as well as* completely embracing the concept of *being* more. Taking more risks, and having more successes, failures, and mistakes. Setting limits and breaking down limitations. Connecting to a deeper knowledge of myself, with compassion and self-love. Getting in touch with my soul and my deeper sense of purpose. Envisioning the best possible life, and then *going for it.*

Living BIG is what you're going to discover in this book. From the practical tips to the soul-challenging questions, this process is one of how to connect with the life you've wished for but haven't dared to dream about.

In the next chapter, I'll introduce you to the EMPOWERS process. The rest of the book will take you through the specifics, one chapter (and concept) at a time. You will learn to access cumulative change through a simple, straightforward process of empowerment that is powerful and transformative.

You can have it all. *It's time.*

Chapter 3
The EMPOWERS Process

"I've learned that people will forget what you said, people will forget what you did, but people will never forget how you made them feel."
Maya Angelou

The EMPOWERS process is designed to support you in moving into a place of happiness and fulfillment, creating a sense of purpose, and finding the time to "have it all."

You know how everyone else (or a lot of other people) seems to live amazing lives, juggling ten thousand things without batting an eye and are always happy? And how you've been wishing that it was *you* doing all those fabulous things and feeling great? The EMPOWERS process is all about how to get you there in a way that uses the skills you already have, and adds in a few new twists, that result in *You, version 2.0.*

You're probably not shocked to learn that a process that's all about getting the life you want is related to empowerment. *Empowerment* means *giving power or authority to*, and that's what we're looking for— ways for *you to give yourself* more power and authority, so you have the life you want. By following the same eight-step EMPOWERS process that Theresa, Bethany, Sandi, and I followed, you will gain access to the *how* of turning things around.

I'll give you a summary of the EMPOWERS process steps here, and then we'll look at each step in more detail in the coming chapters.

E—Enhance Your Energy

You've been running on empty for a long time. You know about the idea of self-care, but you've been too tired to really get anywhere with finding relief. You need some strategies, *fast,* that give quick results so you can start the rest of the process. In the Enhance chapter, we'll discuss ways you can set limits, access additional resources, and determine the truth behind what feels like failure to you. You will also learn a super-cool way to ramp up your energy and get rid of energies that may be holding you back.

When you're in a place of feeling like a hamster on a wheel, or feel like you're taking one step forward and three steps back, it's hard to see that there are choices and options. Enhancing your energy addresses the mindset of scarcity and gives you a chance to recreate the story you've been telling about your life.

M—Make Extra Time

It is possible to create extra time in your life (although I haven't figured out the "more than 24 hour" thing). The short version of how to do it is to prioritize, say no, stop multi-tasking, and start living in the now.

I know—this is where you roll your eyes and say, "Yeah, right. Heard it already—way too many times. Doesn't work." I *absolutely believe* that you have tried and it hasn't worked. I have been in that same place. And I have been super aggravated and frustrated at what felt like the dismissive response of "just do it." But I'm not talking about a same-old, same-old approach to organizing your time. I'm suggesting a deeper look at the differences between obligations and choices, and a more expansive way to understand how you look at the world.

Richard Bach, in his book *Illusions*, made a statement that I have lived by for the last 25 years (not always with total success, but sometimes I'm really stubborn). He wrote, "Argue for your limitations, and sure enough, they're yours." That idea is at the core of Make Extra Time, once you've started the work to Enhance your Energy.

The other half of Make Extra Time is about resting, relaxing, and recharging. It's combining the concepts of mindfulness and meditation, with self-care *and* strong boundaries in relationships. It involves valuing yourself and your connections and making them work *for* you, instead of against you.

P—Practice Perspective

Woohoo! This step is truly the fast-track to happiness. This is where research meets reality, and you start to feel and see a difference. You will learn and practice ways to identify early triggers to stress. You will embrace the gift of frustration and take the concept of choice to a whole new level (the *meta-view*). Using the exercises and suggestions in this chapter, you will become a master of perspective.

Perspective seems like such a simple word. This step of the process involves understanding the straight-up message of "It's not about you, except when it's all about you." And, believe me, that's going to be a huge relief and will bring you so much freedom. You are going to love being in a place of only being responsible for your own feelings, thoughts, and actions.

O—Own Your Best Self

You have a best self. Your best self is amazing. The trouble is, you may not have been hanging out with that part of yourself enough. You're already a great friend to others, but this step is all about learning to be your own best friend. For real. This means utilizing all the compassion and caring you give to others and applying them to yourself. This is where you learn the truth behind self-acceptance, about appreciating the perfection in your imperfection and loving yourself for *exactly who you are*.

Have you listened to the song "Try" by Colbie Callait? Or "Who Says" by Selena Gomez? (Sneak peek: Later on I will share a whole playlist with you that was born from the EMPOWERS process). Both of those songs are about getting in touch with your inner best self and celebrating her. The only way to *have* the life you really want is to *be* the person you really are *and love her fully*.

W—Wake up Your Inner Rock Star

Now we're getting into some super powerful places. This step is about looking at the roles you play in your life and figuring out which are moving you forward and which are holding you back from your total awesome self.

I love the idea of being a rock star. It sounds so powerful, strong, and confident. And that's you. You will hear all about how I waited 18 years to buy the car I *actually* wanted to have (hint: it's yellow) and what kept me from making that small (yet unbelievably empowering) decision. And you will benefit from not having to wait eighteen years to be your own rock star and get what you *actually* want.

I heard a great phrase the other day: "Own what you know" (Danielle Miller said it. She does really cool work with archetypes and business). This step is about finding your voice—your deep-down, true, empowered voice—and using it in all the areas of your life. So, of course, you will be confronting that monster-in-the-closet: *I'm not good enough.* You're going to open the closet door wide, face that monster, and discover it's only a tattered old shirt that didn't get hung up right (and that *really* needs to go in the trash; it's not even fit to donate to Goodwill).

E—Envision Your Inner Purpose

Discovering and *living* your happy, fulfilled life means being connected to your inner purpose, or soul purpose. You have one, even if you don't think you do. That's because we all do. An inner purpose isn't necessarily some big, grand mission. But it *is* something that you are called to do. Because you are called to live this inner purpose, it's world-changing, whether you do or don't live it. Not living your inner purpose deprives everyone, whereas living it spreads the benefits beyond what you can imagine.

Do you remember when our society first became aware of HIV/AIDS? All of a sudden, there were a lot of conversations happening about having safe sex (which was fabulous). What I remember most is the description of how a sexually transmitted disease could spread. It went something like this: "When you have unprotected sex with someone, you are also having sex with everyone they have had sex with and with everyone *those* people have ever had sex with and with..." and on, and on. There was a graphic that started with two people and quickly blossomed out to a community, a city—basically to a ginormous number of people. And you thought you were just having sex with the person next to you!

That's the same impact that living (or not living) your inner purpose has. But it's even more widespread, since you are starting with *every* person you come into contact with. And it spreads to the people they have contact with. And on, and on.

So, connecting to your inner purpose is pretty important. And you're going to have that covered.

R—Release the Blocks and Go for It

There's no getting around this step. For every time you have ever said, "It won't work," "It can't happen," "I'm too tired," or "I don't know how"—this is the answer. You will access the phenomenal power of manifestation and understand how quantum physics gives you a guidebook for creating what's been missing in your life. You will learn the correct use of "What if?" and how to amp up the results you get, which naturally means you will wrangle with self-doubt and win (you're a rock star, remember?).

This is the step where the rubber meets the road. This is when all the work you have done up until now can go spiraling down the drain. This step is about recognizing that fear has a hiding place inside you, and acknowledging that with compassion and conviction.

It doesn't work to run away from fear, because then you can be attacked from behind. It doesn't work to put up your fists and fight fear, because it's too slippery and it shape-shifts. The key to vanquishing the debilitating effects of fear is to embrace it, claim it, and invite it in for dinner (but not for an extended stay). It's not as hard as it might seem, and you will be *so* pumped when you take this step.

S—Shine Your Light Brightly

You made it! This is the last step, the jump off the high diving board into cool, clear, refreshing water. This is the joyous place of putting it all together and rocking it out. This part of the process is all about celebration and ways to keep the party going. This is where you zero in on the songs, words, and images that will sustain, excite, and inspire you.

>>> <<<

Those are the eight steps of the EMPOWERS process. You might be thinking, *No sweat. I've totally got this.* Or you might be feeling somewhat overwhelmed right now, having thoughts that are more like, *That's a lot to do. I might not be able to do all of it.* The good news is that you start with the first step, and doing the first step will already help you with moving on to the next step after that.

In the next chapter, you will learn how to *enhance your energy*, which is the perfect way to kick off your transformation from stressed to happy and fulfilled.

Chapter 4

E—Enhance Your Energy

"Energy is the key to creativity. Energy is the key to life."
William Shatner

D awn came to me for coaching, but at first she wasn't sure if she needed coaching or just to win the lottery so she could have a month in the sun, lying on the beach and sipping fruity drinks with umbrellas (doesn't that sound awesome?). Dawn wanted a magic solution—which meant she wanted to find a way to bend time, so she could get more done. Or to discover a secret mantra, so she would feel happy and satisfied while she ran like a hamster on a wheel. Dawn was a *worker*. Nothing got in the way of meeting her obligations, but it was at a tremendous cost. She felt completely drained of energy and also drained of joy. Some days she fell into bed so exhausted she *couldn't* sleep—but that didn't stop tomorrow from coming, along with a whole new list of things-to-do. She couldn't envision a solution that would address her responsibilities but leave her with enough energy to function.

What she *really* wanted was to stop alternating between feeling like "the Energizer Bunny on crack" and feeling like she was about to drop in her tracks. She wanted to get things done *and* feel good. She wanted to remember that there were roses, and then have time, interest, and energy to smell them (or at least to consider it an option). Dawn told me, "You know that song, Running on Empty? That's my daily life. Whenever I think I might catch up, something else happens and I'm even further behind." You wouldn't know that if you saw what Dawn accomplished every day. She didn't *seem* like someone who was struggling, and that was part of the problem. When she thought about her life, she was proud about what she'd done, but shocked at the fact she was still going. Her perception was that she had accomplished a mountain of tasks, but it was only a tiny little hill in the Himalayas of her life. Her list of responsibilities was endless, yet somehow got bigger every day.

My first (real) question to Dawn was, "How often do you ask for and accept help?" I bet you can guess her answer. She was quick to tell me that "it just isn't an option." *She* was the one responsible for the things she had to do, and even if she could have shared the burden, there wasn't anyone to ask. Dawn was very sensitive to the issue of time, which included other people's time. She didn't want to put anyone else out, and she knew how hard things were for her friends and family, so asking for help was a no-go.

Have you found yourself in a similar place of feeling like you are being sucked dry by the ongoing need to get things done? Drained of energy with no re-charging station in sight? Wishing there was a way, but believing that you are supposed to be *offering* help, not asking for it? I understand that some things are non-negotiable for you (you don't want someone else washing your underwear; you aren't giving your debit card or bank account access information to someone else; you *will* attend your child's soccer game and Christmas concert), but what about the options you might not be considering? What do you do when a friend asks, "Is there anything I can do to help?" Do you answer with "No, I'm all set, but thank you anyway"? How about answering, instead, with "Would you be willing to help me with weeding the garden next Saturday?" or "I'd love to have your company and assistance with clearing out my downstairs closet. It would be faster, and way more fun, if you were there"? When your boss is asking for volunteers to organize the fall charity drive, what compels you to offer even though you've already been juggling the maximum amount of responsibility at work? How about letting a co-worker volunteer instead? Or suggesting to your boss that you would happily spearhead the event, but can your colleague assume some of the big tasks during the charity drive?

This step is a fast-track to conserving your energy and feeling better. Conserving means you have more to use when you want to. Feeling tired and overwhelmed by things that "can't change" is a common theme for the women I work with. It was true for Dawn, and it's been true for me, as well. It wasn't only about not wanting to ask for help. There was also that other ugly area of (eye roll, shudder, grimace) *boundaries*. Not having good boundaries is like quicksand for your energy. The more you struggle, the deeper you sink. The *Merriam-Webster Dictionary* defines *boundary* as *something that indicates or fixes a limit*. Do you know where your limits are? And are you honoring those limits? I am confident that there are several areas in your life that have "fluid" boundaries, meaning you are doing more than you really want to do; you are doing things because you feel you "have to" do them; you are doing it because someone else expects it of you. You've heard this before, most likely, and determined that there *are* no other options, so you "have to" do things the way you've been doing them. *Obviously*, if there was a way for you to do less (and still live with yourself and your personal expectations), you would be doing it. Who wouldn't, right?

Chances are very high that your perception of what is possible and what is necessary has an underlying theme of scarcity. That was true for Dawn—she perceived a scarcity of time, resources, options, and choices. Dawn truly believed she was doing all she could, running as fast as possible, and not ever getting closer to the finish line. Not because she wasn't competent, but because she couldn't *conceive* of a way to do things differently. Dawn had already run through all the possible scenarios that she could conceive of, and—from her perspective—nothing less than divine intervention would make a difference.

Except—*oops*—she was wrong. What Dawn didn't have was a clear picture of her strengths, her limits, or her resources. She had considered each of those areas, as I'm sure you have, but when you are gauging your results based on internalized ideas about what's expected, rather than on fully valuing your own time, attention, and needs, you're going to get a skewed result. It's not always easy to say no. In fact, many people cringe at the *thought* of saying no. But the whole point of having a boundary is that there is a *limit*. You've already discovered that there are more potential activities and responsibilities than can possibly fit into a single day, or into one person's life, so sometimes it's necessary to say no. That was the starting point for Dawn. She began with setting limits on her own negative thoughts and her high internal expectations. She learned to say, "Not right now" when she felt that the only solution was agreeing to do something more. Dawn started enhancing her energy by spending it wisely, on the things that most mattered to her.

The next step in enhancing energy was for Dawn to look at how she defined *failure* and *success* in her life. If she missed getting something done, or tried something new and it didn't go perfectly, she felt like she had failed. That was a major contributor to her feeling tired and drained. She didn't have room for creativity or new ventures, because she didn't want to do anything that didn't go well. I suggested she define *everything* as a success. She was horrified. She had clear ideas of what success and failure meant, and "screwing something up" was never going to be on her success list. She didn't believe she was in charge of whether something ended up in the success or failure category. Is the same true for you? What might happen if you changed your definition of success? There is *so much freedom* to be found there.

Here's an example. Let's say you signed up for a yoga class. You only went to the second class because you'd paid for a series of seven classes. Plus, your daughter went with you, so you wanted to set a good example. The few times you practiced on the Wii at home didn't give you a lot of confidence about your performance. You spent more time falling (and swearing) than you spent successfully doing (any) pose. Your particular nemesis was Tree Pose. It's not natural to stand on one leg with the other foot bent and resting above (not on) your knee. To say you were experiencing trepidation is an understatement, but you soldiered on. Within the first ten minutes of the hour-long class you had already fallen behind (and fallen down). As you took a quick break in Child's Pose you glanced around at all the other amazing, flexible, talented, balance-gifted members of the class and you *knew* you were a total failure at yoga. Whose stupid idea was it to even try? Then you caught the last little part of a sentence by the yoga instructor and tuned back in to what she was saying: "It's called yoga *practice*, not yoga *perfect*. Remember to breathe and appreciate that you showed up on your mat to practice. That's what it's all about." Hang on. Was she talking to *you*? Did she somehow know what was going on in your head? Or did you (God forbid), start talking out loud?

That's a true story from my life (surprise). It was one of the most profound personal realizations of my life. When I stopped berating myself and looking at how I was "failing," I developed a whole new way to define success. If I'm genuinely trying, authentically giving it my best, then I call it a success. Regardless of the outcome. Because whether or not I can do Tree Pose (I did finally master it, most days), I'm learning something about myself in the process. Making it through a yoga class isn't the same as not getting a promotion or losing a friend. And yet *it is*, in the most fundamental, fabulous way. When you give yourself credit for showing up, when you value your effort, when you take the risk, you are succeeding at *living your life*. You know how this works—when you have a success, you have more energy.

You might be more used to attending to "big" successes (and telling yourself that you haven't had as many as you want). There's another way to approach this. Celebrate your success in the little things, as well as the big ones. Did you manage to go for a walk today? Hooray! Did you finish that (almost overdue) assignment at work? Woohoo! Did you remember to eat lunch before you developed a migraine and almost passed out? You go, girl! This isn't a case of over-praising or watering down your expectations. This is about recognizing the effort and energy you put into all you do, and making sure you are *noticing* those things.

Try This

Pick one day (how about today?) and notice how you feel first thing in the morning. Throughout the day, pay attention to what you are doing and celebrate every single accomplishment. You don't have to break out into song, but a virtual (or real) pat on the back is totally appropriate. Make sure you are including the mundane (*Wow. I made time to go to the bathroom today*). At the end of the day, notice how you feel. See if you can pinpoint the parts of your day that felt better and that felt *energized*. You likely noticed a trend of feeling better whenever you paid attention to the success rather than the failure (*I ate my lunch* vs. *I had to wolf down my lunch because I was running late*). This is one of those exercises that needs a *lot* of practice. So—practice.

Secret Weapon—Chakras

The strategies of asking for help and setting boundaries worked for Dawn. She gradually began to shift her definition of success to a focus on what was working, or what she had learned during a process. Amazingly (to Dawn), her energy was increasing. She started to sleep better and wake up looking forward to the day (or at least not dreading it). She felt like she was off the hamster wheel and starting to move forward. But she still had too many times of feeling like she was in a maze and running into dead ends. She needed something more, something to help her power up when necessary, and also power down, so she didn't drain her batteries. Luckily, there was a *secret weapon* for enhancing her energy.

Are you familiar with the chakras? Chakras are centers of energy flow in the body. You may have heard of the seven chakras, which range from the first chakra at the base of the spine (root chakra) to the seventh chakra, on the top of the head (crown chakra). The second chakra is the sacral chakra (about three fingers below your belly button). The third chakra is the solar plexus chakra (found at your solar plexus, about three inches above your belly button). Your heart chakra is the fourth chakra (at the center of your breastbone). The hollow of your throat is the place of the fifth (throat) chakra. The sixth chakra is in between and just above your eyes (your "third eye"). Each chakra is associated with a color, ranging from red (root chakra) to violet (crown chakra). You can remember this by the letters ROYGBIV, which stands for red-orange-yellow-green-blue-indigo-violet. Each chakra is connected to a function of your body/mind/emotions/spirit.

The root (first) chakra represents your foundation and being grounded. The second (sacral) chakra is associated with the physical body, sexuality, abundance, well-being and pleasure. The third (solar plexus) chakra is the area dealing with your sense of self: self-esteem, self-worth, self-confidence. Your heart chakra (fourth) is about love, inner peace, and relationships. The fifth chakra (throat) is associated with communication, speaking up, and self-expression. Your third eye (sixth chakra) represents the areas of insight, intuition, inner knowing, and imagination. The seventh (crown) chakra is your connection to spirituality and inner and outer beauty.

You can check your chakras by paying close attention to the energy associated with each of the chakra points. If you are sensitive to feeling energy through your hands, you can hold a hand over any of the chakras and assess whether the energy there feels loose and flowing, or if you notice stagnant energy or blockage.

Another way of checking your chakras is by using a pendulum or a crystal. To do this, first work with a pendulum or crystal to get a sense of the motion associated with clear or open energy, and what direction/ motion signifies heavy or stuck energy. Often, clockwise motion is an indicator of balanced, open chakras. Similarly, a counter-clockwise direction may be a sign of heavy energy or energy that is preventing you from fully living your life. When the pendulum is motionless, that's a pretty strong sign that there's some "gunk in the works," or some issues that need to be addressed. Hold your hand, or your pendulum, over each of the chakra points, one by one. Notice what kind of energetic response you get. If the energy feels calm and even, and has a regular flow, that's super. Go on to the next chakra. If the energy feels frenetic, or stagnant and stuck, then it's time to clear that energy out.

Try This

Sit or lie down in a comfortable position (it can be super awesome to try this while taking an Epsom salt bath). Take three slow, deep breaths. Starting with your root chakra (red), breathe in while you visualize the chakra as a spinning red wheel. As you breathe out, imagine the red becoming more and more vibrant. With each exhale, visualize your root chakra become brighter and clearer, to the point of the color being strong and transparent (a dull, muddy or dark color means there's still some clearing to do). Once you feel you've envisioned this as well as possible, move on to the next chakra. Go through each chakra, with its associated color (ROYGBIV), keeping your breathing full and regular. After you've finished with the crown chakra (violet), congrats! Celebrate. Keep in mind that the state of your chakras varies over time—even during the course of a day.

Dawn *loved* learning about her chakras. She realized she could do a quick chakra visualization during her lunch break, or before bed. Presto chango. She didn't feel as bogged down internally and was less likely to see herself as caught in a maze. Dawn even bought an orange stone that she carried around with her as a reminder to allow herself the opportunity to let go and take a break or ask for help. The orange represented her second chakra—her physical body and her basic drives, which were usually the first to be forgotten when she got overwhelmed. Her favorite saying became, *Breathe in the good stuff and breathe out the bad stuff.* That's an awesome way to remember how important it is to focus on our breathing and be intentional about letting things go.

Dawn was tuned in to her own energy, and that gave her a quick way to assess what she needed and when. When she combined this with better boundaries (and viewing asking for help as a success), she was as productive but a lot happier.

During our last session, Dawn laughed as she reminisced about her initial wish to escape her life for a month. She told me that instead of needing to run away, or collapse, in order to stop the merry-go-round, she was now choosing her own carnival rides and deciding when she got off or on. She wasn't tired all the time, and she was loving the smell of roses. She had also taken an amazing vacation to a sunny tropical beach, and she had been thrilled to have the energy to *enjoy* the experience instead of sleeping through it.

Dawn's results *are* typical, and they are *absolutely achievable.* If you're wondering how long it will be before you can expect results, I have great news for you. If you make a commitment to yourself to embrace the idea of asking for and accepting help for one week, you will see a noticeable change in your energy level. On every day that you notice and acknowledge your new definition of success, you will build your bank account of energy. It's like an interest-bearing savings account, with your automatic deposits of self-recognition and appreciation growing exponentially and being available for days when you need to make a larger withdrawal to deal with your life's circumstances.

Are you afraid you won't have enough time to enhance your energy? The EMPOWER process has you covered. In the next chapter, Make More Time, we'll focus on creating space for things that are necessary as well for what you love. Sneak peek: It's *not* about being a better multi-tasker.

Chapter 5
M—Make More Time

"Argue for your limitations, and sure enough, they're yours."
Richard Bach, Illusions

Richard Bach's words, above, are incredibly powerful, and that cause and effect has likely figured somewhere in your life story. Remember Theresa, who absolutely *knew* that juggling full-time work, three school-age children, a husband, and a house meant that she could never even *imagine* achieving her dream of getting her doctorate? She was positive she didn't even have the time to *think* about it, never mind apply to a program. There was truth behind her beliefs. Maybe not the whole truth, but she *was* very, very busy. So busy she didn't have time for herself—not to exercise, not to see friends, not for date night with her husband.

39

When Theresa and I first started to look at her dreams and what she wanted from her life, all she said she really wanted was "more time." She said she wanted *more time to do more of the things she was already doing*. Although she loved (most of) her job, and absolutely loved her family and house, she didn't ever feel she was caught up with all there was to do. So, even though somewhere in the back of her mind a little voice was saying, *What about me? What about my goals and dreams?* that wasn't the voice she was listening to when she thought about more time. Instead, she kept hearing the voice that said, *You need to get it all done. Other women do this all the time. Why can't you figure this out? What is wrong with you?*

Can you guess where that negative train of thought led to? Perhaps you've had one or two of those thoughts yourself, so you already know. Theresa's thinking led her in circles, creating a powerful downward spiral. She went faster and faster, trying to do more and more, all the while hearing the internal voice that said, *You aren't doing enough. You still have to do blah blah blah. You will never get it all done* (it doesn't even matter what the specifics were—the message was the same, regardless of circumstances). Worse, Theresa felt inadequate, discouraged, and hopeless. She was falling off the treadmill of her life and didn't know how to make a change that would slow life down enough for her to do something different. Somehow, the speed was ramping up, and she was breathless, with no end in sight. It felt to her like the treadmill was perched on a cliff and one wrong move, one slower step, and she would plunge over the edge.

Multi-Tasking

How was Theresa trying to handle the overwhelm? First, she tried to master multi-tasking. While driving to work, she would create a list of everything she had to do that day. When the mental list wasn't sufficient, she started to dictate into her phone (hands-free, of course).

Soon she was creating categories and folders within her to-do list. When she got to work, she highlighted the items that were "must do"—and when she realized there were more must-dos than time in the day, that usually made her remember two or three more imperative tasks. She ate lunch (when she felt she could fit it in at all) while doing work-related reading and responding to emails. She fielded constant interruptions during the day, in order to remain accessible to her staff. At the end of the workday, which was always at least an hour later than anyone else left, she quickly packed up all the work she hadn't gotten to, and rushed to get to her next task. Phone calls were returned while she was grocery shopping. While cooking dinner, she helped the kids with homework, glanced at the mail (bills, naturally), and fantasized about going to bed instead of attacking the mountain of work she'd brought home. After dinner, cleaning up the dishes, and getting the kids ready for bed, she would sit in the family room with her husband, the television, and her briefcase full of work. They talked during commercials, reviewing their days and what they had going on for the coming weekend—who was driving to hockey practice, how many basketball games there were to attend, who was going to pick up the birthday present for the party their daughter was going to, who was going to get stuck helping to supervise twelve to fifteen energetic six-year-olds at Bounce Town. Theresa felt overwhelmed by all she and her husband had to manage but was also grateful she wasn't doing it alone. It was already impossible, even with two people. After an hour or so, she would pack up the work she still needed to complete, send herself reminder emails for the next day, and stagger off to bed.

Although Theresa was becoming adept at juggling, she was missing one of the most important truths about her time management approach: *Multi-tasking doesn't work.* Multi-tasking results in doing many things partially, without full attention. Multi-tasking means nothing gets done as well as it could. Worst of all, multi-tasking takes *more* time, overall, rather than less time. Crazy, right? I personally struggled with grasping this concept. It seemed to me that if I could do several things at once, I was being *efficient*. I was really using every moment to it's full potential. Nope. When you're paying partial attention, you work more slowly. Your brain is trying to do too many things at once, with a finite store of energy, so everything has to slow down some in way so that you can spread the limited energy across the various tasks. The other thing that happens is that you, therefore, miss details. Those details may not be life or death kinds of situations, but there's a very high probability the missing details will require you to re-do, or return to, some part of the task. *This takes extra time*—more time than you would have spent if you hadn't been multi-tasking to start with. Truth.

Try This

Whenever I start to feel frenetic, or when the urge to start multi-tasking like a madwoman comes over me, I repeat one of these two phrases to myself: *A stitch in time saves nine* or *Haste makes waste*. I know, really old school. But it's effective. I've found I need a concrete phrase or action to remind me to switch out of hamster-on-the-wheel mode and back into making a conscious choice about how I spend my time and energy. If those phrases don't work for you, come up with your own. You can play around with this and develop two or three words or phrases that will trigger the same message to stop and regroup, and do one thing at a time. Try the phrases one at a time for at least a couple of days. It works. You'll see.

Prioritizing

Now that you have a strategy to help you stop multi-tasking, you can combine it with a few other steps. First up is prioritizing. I assume you have been using this strategy for years, and that what it's led to is multi-tasking. Not any more. When you create your priority list, make sure you switch it up by taking five minutes to determine a *working* prioritization. This is going to save you tons of time.

What do I mean by a "*working* prioritization"? In the past, you probably set your priorities according to either what had to be done, noting the earliest possible date, or the biggest task you absolutely *must* complete during the time frame you were prioritizing about. While both are decent strategies, they don't fall into the "Wow, I actually saved time" category. What works better is assessing your time commitment, the drop-dead date, *and* the ease of task completion. When you take all three of those factors into consideration, you are going to get a different list of things to do. Have you ever wondered why classes in high school are usually limited to an hour, sometimes an hour and a half? Or why college or grad school classes offer a break halfway through a three-hour class? It's because there's a limit to how long we can effectively concentrate in a single sitting. This applies to your schedule as well. (Of course, if you are in "flow" and really in the groove with something, time can seem to fade away and you might work longer with good effect. But I bet a lot of the things on your must-do list aren't activities that completely engage your interest and bring you joy.)

Assess how long it will take to complete each item you're considering prioritizing. You don't need to make another list (that's only procrastination). Simply scan or review to get a general idea of what's most time-consuming. Then take a second look and determine which items *really* need to be done right away (the assignment from your boss might be due tomorrow, but if you don't call the school today to schedule the parent-teacher conference, the only times left will be impossible to fit into your schedule, so that's leading the must-do ASAP group). Review the list one more time to assess what can be done easily and simply. This is super important, because whenever you complete an item, you get a feeling of accomplishment. Make sure you're building in opportunities to experience success—it will give you a little energy boost and make the rest of the list easier to approach.

Now that you know the time frames, the degree of urgency, and the level of difficulty—mix them up. Don't plan to spend all day completing one report—you will get discouraged and your productivity will decrease. I recently spoke to a college student who told me she'd studied twelve hours in a row for a test. Way too long. She didn't plan in breaks, and spent most of the time worrying about not having enough time and not being able to do enough. To switch it up, she developed a strategy of studying for two hours, then taking a minimum half-hour break. She also planned in meals, instead of skipping lunch altogether or only eating junk food. She discovered that each time she returned to her work she was better able to focus and got a lot more done. This method works for managing responsibilities at home, work, and school. In addition, you can plan to include some of the easily accomplished items during your break time. But don't skip meals—there's no sense in draining your battery.

You may already be doing some of this without recognizing it as a specific strategy. It's kind of like that time your in-laws were due for dinner, the house was a mess, you needed to get groceries, and you hadn't done laundry in over a week. Oh, and cleaning the bathroom was an absolute must. You threw the laundry in the washer, focused on the bathroom, and got it done just in time to put the clothes in the dryer (you knew they could stay there—what houseguest looks in the dryer?). Vacuuming didn't take much time, so you got that out of the way. Off you went to the grocery store (you needed to get out of the house by then, and getting ready to go was a great excuse to take a shower while you still had time). Maybe you even picked up a few extra items while you were out and talked for a few minutes with the friend you saw in the frozen food section. Back home you put the lasagna together and, after it was in the oven, you realized that if you closed your child's bedroom door to hide the mess, you could sit and relax. And you did. Prioritization and no multi-talking. Successful completion of tasks, *and* time to play on Pinterest. *You're a superstar.*

Certainly, you could have arranged the day differently—but by getting an overview of what you needed to do, and alternating the tasks while paying attention to estimated time-to-completion, it *worked.* Besides preparing for your dinner company, you also used the second major step for gaining more time: *You said no to some things* (in this case, folding and putting away the laundry and trying to wade through the disaster area that was your child's bedroom).

Sure, at some point the laundry has to be dealt with—but it doesn't have to be *now.* And maybe you can assign that chore to someone else. This is a vital principle. Not only is it okay to *not* do everything, but also you can say no and still be a phenomenal woman. Really successful, *happy* women make a practice of saying no. They say no to being on another committee at work. They say no to being the organizer of the PTO fundraiser for the fourth year in a row. They say no (or not right now) to requests to volunteer at church, synagogue, school, and book club (especially when they haven't had the time or energy to read the book). In addition to saying no, *they also say yes.* Yes to taking a bath. Yes to going to the gym or a yoga class. Yes to getting pizza instead of cooking dinner. Yes to coffee with a friend before heading home.

This is a two-part strategy of realizing you don't have to accept every invitation to dance, and *choosing* what you want to do. In this way, you come to understand that your worth as a person, a colleague, a mother, and a partner is *not* based on how often you say yes to other people's requests. Fully stepping into saying no to the things that feel like one more obligation and saying yes to activities that enhance your life is the same underlying principle as how you organize your to-do list. You make sure there are opportunities for what energizes you, and decrease time spent on what doesn't. We can get caught up in a feeling of obligation—the *should dos* taking precedence over the *I want tos*. I'm not suggesting you never do something you feel is less-than-exciting even though it's the "right" thing to do. This is about seeing the difference between obligation and choice, and making sure your decisions are not overly weighted on the side of obligation. The very best way to manage obligations is to sandwich them with activities that are rewarding (and hopefully fun). When you tell your child (and mean it) that she has to clean her room before you take her to the amusement park, you present her with a reward for accomplishing an obligatory task. It works.

Recharge

Following these guidelines will save time and start to make a dent in the feelings of never catching up, but it's not enough. You must also do what allows you to rest, relax, and re-charge. This is non-optional if you really want to have extra time. Just like your body needs fuel to keep running (the reason it's important to not skip meals when you're busy), your mind and spirit need opportunities to rejuvenate. This is why saying yes to fun, enjoyable activities is as important as being able to say no to things that are not a priority. You have probably been saying no to *yourself* and saying yes to meeting the needs of other people. *This has got to change.*

When I fly, I love to hear flight attendants tell me to put my oxygen mask on first. It's the only part of the pre-flight spiel I actually listen to. But every time I hear them say this, I am reminded that we can't take care of someone else if we haven't taken care of ourselves. You probably do this a lot. Meet the needs (or demands) of job, family, community. And it's a pretty safe bet that you tell yourself something like, *Well, it really needs to get done* or *It's a good cause* or *I can just cancel... (seeing friends, "me" time, etc.).* Often, we don't even realize how low our batteries are until we just drop. Maybe you keep saying yes to others (and no to yourself) until you get sick. Or until you literally can't do anything and you *have to* cancel everything. Or until you become so irritable and frustrated, you are sick of being around yourself. There's no reason it has to get this bad, and yet we do it over and over again. We do it because we have an unequal balance of yes and no when it comes to ourselves. But if you follow the flight attendant's advice, you will make sure to include yourself in the group of people whose needs you are trying to meet. And guess what? When you take care of yourself on a regular and timely basis, you have more energy. You go about your day with a little more bounce in your step. You are more efficient. *You are creating extra time.* There are still twenty-four hours in the day, but you're not dragging through them at half-speed, because you've been giving all your life-sustaining energy away. Instead, you are giving yourself the chance to refuel. And refueling means you have something to share. It's a positive feedback loop, and it works to everyone's benefit.

As you consider how you want to recharge, I strongly suggest you consider two areas in particular: *nurturing your relationships* and *mindfulness.* Connections to people who matter are vitally important in our lives. There is no substitute for a smile or a hug from someone who really gets you. The power of laughing and sharing is amazing. Have you ever heard the saying "A burden shared is a burden halved"? There's so much truth in that statement. That doesn't mean you want all your interpersonal interactions to be focused around what's going wrong, or on defining your burdens. But it does mean there's a form of *release* and *relief* in being able to share your inner self with someone else—the good, the bad, the mundane, and the ordinary. If you are in a committed relationship, that's certainly a bond worthy of paying attention to. It's also worthwhile to grow your associations and linkages to people outside your primary relationship (you know—friends). Both types of relationships are valuable, and they provide different kinds of support. So, leverage connections with your friends into win-win situations— your friends get the benefit of time with your fabulous self, you get to soak up their awesomeness, and everyone has the chance to recharge their flagging batteries.

Mindfulness

"Mindfulness is about being fully awake in our lives. It is about perceiving the exquisite vividness of each moment. We also gain immediate access to our own powerful inner resources for insight, transformation, and healing."
Jon Kabat-Zinn

Jon Kabat-Zinn is a well-known teacher, researcher, author, and practitioner of mindfulness. He founded the program Mindfulness Based Stress Reduction at the University of Massachusetts Medical School and has written countless books, articles, and scientific papers on mindful living. I love his description of mindfulness as being "fully awake." Mindfulness is the antithesis of multi-tasking, by definition. It's when you are completely involved in what you are doing and *paying attention* while you are doing it. You know those conversations with someone when, in the middle of you saying something, the other person seems to zone out and you can tell they are not really listening to you? It doesn't matter if they are internally planning their next statement, developing a rebuttal, composing a shopping list, or saying a prayer. What you notice is they are no longer in the moment with you. The whole interaction loses some of its shine, at least for a moment. They have stopped being mindful, stopped being *present*, and you can tell. On the other hand, think about those times when you have seen a dedicated performer—maybe a pianist or a guitarist—up on stage playing in front of a huge crowd, and just by looking at them you know nothing exists for them in that moment but the music. That creates a powerful experience.

When you are living with full attention in the present moment, you are practicing mindfulness (and it usually takes a *lot* of practice). Our minds love to meander, and they naturally start wandering away from what we're doing unless we are totally engaged. You know that feeling of getting so caught up in an experience you don't notice time is passing—that's being mindful; and you also know what it's like to feel time crawling so slowly you want to scream. Since this chapter is about time, mindfulness is a prime tool.

The way to learn mindfulness usually starts with breathing and observation. When you slow down and truly notice what you are doing and what's going on, you become more aware of your feelings and the sensations in your body. You live in the present, and all the worries, concerns, and to-dos no longer occupy your attention. It's like pushing the pause button, and it gives your internal self an opportunity to step off the treadmill without falling. It's revitalizing to stop running as fast as you can.

When Theresa was at the point of complete exhaustion and plumb out of ideas, she made the commitment to the practice of making more time. As we discussed mindfulness and the ways in which she could experiment with it, I introduced her to a few basic yoga poses—poses she could do anywhere—at work, in the car, at home, by the pool. They were poses that matched simple movements with her breath, helping her focus on her breathing and be in the present moment. Theresa gave it a shot, and then couldn't wait to share the fantastic news—"Guess what? I took ten minutes in the morning to do those yoga poses. I didn't really think it was going to do anything other than make me late for work, but I tried. And just as I was finishing, the most amazing thing happened. I noticed that I had actually relaxed and stopped adding to my inner list of things to do. The ten-minute timer went off, and I was shocked that ten minutes was up, but I was even more shocked at how *calm* I felt." Theresa was so thrilled with the results that she kept it up, and soon noticed that she was getting a lot more done. Imagine that.

> *"If you want to conquer the anxiety of life,*
> *live in the moment, live in the breath."*
> **Amit Ray**

Try This

Find a comfortable place to sit and set a timer for ten minutes (if that feels too long, set it for five minutes; start where you can). Begin to bring your attention to your breath. Notice your inhale. Notice your exhale. Notice the cool air coming in, and notice how it feels going out. Bring your attention to your belly. Notice the rise and fall of your belly as you breathe. Keep breathing and noticing until the timer goes off. Then notice how you feel—no judgment, only observation. Congratulations. *You have just done a mindfulness practice.*

If you want to take it up a notch, start that exercise with a small piece of something edible in your hand (raisins and grapes are common for this exercise. I like to use a Starburst. Whatever works for you is fine). Start the breathing exercise and then bring your attention to observing your edible object. Notice everything about it—the shape, the texture, the temperature, the feeling of it in your hand. Next, put it in your mouth and follow the same pattern of noticing. Pay attention to how it feels in your mouth, its taste, weight, and texture. You will probably notice that the sensations are stronger and more vivid by then (this is the same concept that's behind eating slowly and chewing your food thoroughly before swallowing: you experience the taste more intensely and you also fill up sooner). If you want to go one step further during this meditation, chew as slowly and as many times as possible. Notice what sensations you experience now. You will be amazed at how long one raisin (or one Starburst) can last.

Look at you. Practicing mindfulness and being in the present moment (despite your initial belief that this works for everyone *but* you). Even better, you didn't need to climb a mountain, take a month off to study, or wear special clothing, (although if those are things you enjoy—go for it. This is about you paying attention to and honoring your preferences). You may have noticed that enhancing your energy and making more time get super-charged when you add in a dash of mindfulness. Although you can go through this book in any order, the chapters are designed to build upon each skill, so you're always leveling up in a natural progression.

Practicing Perspective is the focus of the next chapter. It's one of my favorites, because it's all about increasing happiness. What would it be like to have more happiness (and fun) than you can imagine, and all the time and energy, to really experience it?

Chapter 6

P—Practice Perspective

"Happiness cannot be traveled to, owned, earned, worn or consumed. Happiness is the spiritual experience of living every minute with love, grace and gratitude."
Denis Waitley

How often do you find yourself thinking, *Oh, I am so happy?* I hope it's often. But there's a good chance it isn't happening nearly as much as you want, or else you wouldn't be here. The point of this chapter is to give you some workable tips and suggestions so that you can actually *be* happy. To do this, it makes sense to talk about what *blocks* happiness.

What are the things that get in the way of you being happy? I bet they include at least a few of these thoughts:

- *I've got too much to do.*
- *I never have enough time.*
- *I'm tired, and sick of being tired.*
- *I feel stuck.*
- *I feel like something's missing in my life.*
- *I'm stressed.*

Stress

Stress is probably the biggest issue getting in the way of being happy, so let's start with that one. In Chapter 1, we talked about stress and the problems it can cause you, physically, emotionally, and spiritually (because living a stress-filled life is soul-sucking), and the automatic, instinctive response you have to stress. The trick is to figure out how to disarm the stress alarm, by doing something different as soon as it *starts* ramping up. For this to work, you have to notice what's happening. So, what can you use for an early warning system? How can you stop the stress train before it leaves the station, or at least put on the brakes before it totally jumps the tracks?

There are a lot of awesome techniques, but the most vital one is to notice what's going on *in your body*. No fancy tools needed for this one. If you start paying attention to the messages your body is sending you, you already have a step up on the situation. No matter how true it sometimes seems to be, *you do not go from zero to 60* in a heartbeat unless there is a real, unexpected danger. Are you about to become a tasty morsel for a tiger? That's a real danger. Are you about to be sideswiped into oblivion on the highway? That's a real danger, too. Do you have too many things to do before you finally get to go home tonight? Nope, not a real danger. Even though your brain is responding as if your existence is at stake, it's not. That's not to say there isn't a possibility of negative consequences. If you don't get the mortgage payment mailed, you're looking at a late fee, or maybe a negative mark on your credit rating. That's a concern, but it's not immediately life-threatening, *even though it feels like it.*

The kind of stress that *seems* like it's going to drown you if you don't get it all done doesn't come on all at once. It builds up, one little thought at a time. As you're creating the mental list of what you have to do, your body is starting to respond. For the first item, maybe your only reaction is to make a mental note. For the second, third, and fourth items, your muscles begin to tense up. Your shoulders are starting to take up residence next to your ears. Your lower back is tightening. Add in the fifth and sixth items and your stomach growls (sort of like that tiger). By the time you've added items seven, eight, nine, and ten, you can feel the first twinges of a headache and you maybe even feel a little nauseous. The process keeps on going, with more and bigger reactions in your body.

Granted, this whole response might have occurred over the course of one or two minutes, but it didn't happen in the blink of an eye. Go back and read the preceding paragraph again, and see if you can figure out when *you* get a first early warning sign in a similar situation. Chances are, you've become so habituated to this process that you don't notice what's happening until the black cloud of despair rolls in, right along with the thought *This is impossible*, and the onset of a full-blown stress attack. The good news is, there are a lot of signals you can train yourself to notice in order to stop the process before it gets out of hand.

Try This

Bring your attention to your shoulders. Consciously drop them down. Do it again. Do you feel the difference? You're so used to living in a world of non-stop stress that you are almost always prepared to jump into fight-flight-or-freeze mode. You start to tense your muscles without even knowing it's happening. That's what happens when you spend your days battle-ready before there's even a war going on. The act of paying attention to your body, in this case to your shoulders, brings you back to an awareness of the present moment. It sends a tiny signal to your brain that the car is not about to go off the road. And that's what delays the major alarms from being set off. Most importantly, if you can pay attention to what's going on in your body, the thinking part of your brain has a chance to weigh in and assess the situation, rather than automatically triggering the alarm bells.

Try This

Bring your attention to your shoulders. I know, you just did this. But I bet they started creeping up again (force of habit). So, drop your shoulders again. Now see if you can lower your shoulders even more (how low can you go?). This time, purposefully squeeze your shoulders up as high as possible and hold this position for about four seconds. Put them up so high that your neck feels a little sore and is all squished together. Then release your shoulders. And then move them even lower. Following all of these directions gets your brain thinking and too busy to be able to flash those lights and sirens.

Breathing

As much as you want to roll your eyes right now and tell me breathing practices don't work for you—hang in here with me. There's so much evidence about the positive effects of breathing on stress and anxiety that it's not even worth repeating here. You've heard it before, and you've probably even tried it. You've likely had an experience of "breathing" and then telling anyone who will listen that it's a useless technique that doesn't do anything to improve the situation except stress you out even more. Let's look at that more closely.

What we're talking about here is not the average, everyday, automatic breathing that keeps you alive, even when you sleep. Frankly, that's going to happen whether you are trying to breathe or not. This is about slowing down to take a few breaths in a specific pattern. This makes a difference to your body (and, therefore, to your brain), whether or not you "believe" in it. Sending a burst of oxygen to your brain helps clear out the stress fog that prevents you from thinking. Breathing in a specific pattern requires concentration and ensures that your thinking brain is engaged (remember—that means the alarmist in the middle of your brain doesn't get to do it's *Danger! Danger!* thing). When we're stressed, we usually take shallow breaths, breathing from our shoulders. Breathing the right way involves expanding the lungs and diaphragm without using the shoulders.

Try This

Sit in a comfortable, upright position. Place one hand on your belly and the other on your chest. Close your eyes and breathe normally. Pay attention to the rise and fall of your chest and how the air feels in your lungs. Now breathe in for a count of four. Hold your breath for a count of four. Breathe out for a count of four. Pause for a count of four. Repeat this three times.

Now that you know how to breathe, *you have to practice it.* Because a reason that breathing hasn't worked for you is probably that you haven't practiced enough to be able to truly follow those directions *when you are heading for a meltdown.* You may have tried to take a deep breath and count to ten, but unless you were really committed to calming down those internal systems, it didn't work for you. That's because you weren't really giving your thinking brain a chance to reengage, and your amygdala was too busy hitting all the alarms to pay attention. So you have to practice. A lot. Practice this when you *aren't* stressed, if you want it to work when you *are* stressed. It takes less than five minutes, and you can do it absolutely anywhere. If you don't practice, you will keep feeling stressed, and you will continue to believe breathing exercises don't work.

Frustration

How often do you run into situations that are really frustrating and that bring you down? The kind of experience that has you wanting to swear or stamp your foot. Like when you're running late to a meeting and you spill coffee on your shirt. And then you find out that you forgot to pay an important bill (even though there's money in your account), and you have no more dog food at home, so you have to make *another* stop before the day is over. I'm guessing that you've had more than a few of those kinds of days. The key is in *what you do when everything seems to be blowing up around you.*

I was recently listening to the audiobook *You Are A Badass*, by Jen Sincero. It's great, and she has lots of wonderful things to say. I was listening on my iPad while I making an appetizer, so my attention was split between her words and chopping vegetables. And then she said something that made me put down my knife, press rewind, and seriously pay attention. She was talking about having "one of those days" and she went on to say, "This is good because…"

The phrase caught my attention right away. I'm generally a positive person, and I'm pretty skilled at seeing the silver lining in the cloud, so it wasn't a completely new concept. What really blew me away was the power of the affirmative statement. *This* is *good because…* Not *This might be okay because* or *This will be okay because*, or any other trying-to-see-the-good phrase. It was a full-blown, *own it, be it, live it* kind of statement. There was no *try*. Only a *this* is *good.*

What Jen Sincero is advocating is changing your perspective. It can be very challenging to shift a perspective, especially when you're running into obstacles or delays. Let's face it, much of the time your efforts to think differently are half-hearted. You aren't convinced there's an upside to what's going on. The more problematic or intense the situation, the harder it is to look on the bright side, because there doesn't seem to be one.

And yet, every coin has two sides. Literally. We don't live in a one-dimensional world, so there's always *at least* one other side to whatever is going on. It's the yin and yang of our existence. There's always another point of view, even when we can't see past what's right in front of us. The trick is to get outside of the situation, or above it—to tap into the *meta view* that isn't blocked by our emotions.

Getting to a *meta view* means seeing the forest rather than the trees. It's like going up in a plane and then looking out the window at the place you just left. Everything looks so small, like toy villages and Matchbox cars. You see the whole landscape, not only what was visible from your car as you drove to the airport. Maybe you see a traffic jam on the highway, but you can also see beyond the accident to the clear roads leading out of town.

Have you ever looked out from a plane and tried to find a familiar landmark? It all looks so different from way up there. Suddenly, you realize that however big (or small) your house is, it's only one building in a whole bunch of buildings. You get a sense of where you fit in. Look at the situation that's got you all bent out of shape, then imagine looking down on it as if you were in a plane. There's a good chance you'll see more of the landscape. You have the *opportunity* to see what other pieces might be part of this pie. What have you not (yet) considered as part of this situation? What else might be going on? What benefit is there in this situation that wasn't visible from your street-level point of view?

This is more than giving things a positive spin. This is an exercise in taking charge of your perspective, your happiness, and your life. Happiness is a choice. It's matter of making a deliberate selection. My business card says on the back, "Happiness is a choice—it's work, but it's a choice." This is a motto to live your life by, one that I purposefully put in a place where I see it every time I see one of my business cards. I want to see it, not so I can skip through every moment along with the puppies and rainbows, but because I need the reminder—as many of us do—that *I am in charge of how I view the world.*

Choice

There may not be a lot that you can say you are definitely, fully, and completely in charge of. But there is one thing that you *are* in charge of that *no one else in the world can control.* You, and only you, are in charge of your thoughts, feelings, and actions. No matter what someone else says, does, or thinks, they are not in control of your thoughts, feelings, or actions. Also, you are *only* in charge of your own thoughts, feelings, and actions. No matter how badly you may want to, you cannot control anyone else's thoughts, feelings, or actions. Regardless of the situation, there is only one person who can create a thought, feeling, or action in you, and that's you. Someone may influence your choices or your perspective, but you have the control.

By taking a *meta view* of the situation, you step into the power of the moment and understand that your vision is determined by what you *choose* to see. Making sure that you have a wide-angle perspective gives you a lot more choices than you may have imagined were possible. This is true even if your life feels like a permanently cloudy day.

We all have those grey days—days when nothing seems to be going right, including job, home, relationship, and even the weather; days when we're absolutely convinced that the sun will never shine again, at least not where we are. Does this need to be a permanent state? No.

Your view of life, and your circumstances, are what determine your level of happiness. The determiner is not necessarily the actual details of what's going on. Although having money can make some things easier, it's not what brings and maintains happiness. The same is true for a relationship or a job—it's not whether you are in a perfect relationship or have dream perfect job (although both of those are possible) that makes you happy, *What makes you happy is how you view yourself and your life.*

A perspective is like a pair of sunglasses. You can choose any color of lens, from super dark black, through grey, brown, or orange—up to yellow or rose. Yup, rose-colored glasses. You might think the idea of willingly putting on rose-colored glasses is ridiculous and too pie-in-the-sky. Maybe you think the idea of rose-colored glasses isn't based in reality (as if reality is only dark and gloomy).

Sure, you've had (and will continue to have) lots of difficult and challenging moments in your life. There are times when people let you down, when you feel stuck, when you're not able to move forward, when you think happiness is nothing more than an unachievable dream. Even then, happiness is a choice. You can *choose* to focus on the big long list of what is wrong, or you can *choose* to see what opportunities are available and waiting for you to notice. You can *choose* to look for the good thing. Every circumstance holds the possibility of new learning and new growth, but you must be *willing* to see it.

It's Not About You

Now that you are thinking in terms of perspective, here's some even better news: *It's not about you.* Did you ever worry about a pimple when you were in high school? The kind of pimple that seemed to stick out from your face about a mile, was as red as Rudolph's nose, and glowed in the same way? (If you didn't ever have this experience, you are luckier than you know.) That pimple had you convinced that complete and total social ruin was one heartbeat away. You *knew* that as soon as your pimple preceded you into school, your life would be over. Sure, you mother tried to tell you that no one would notice, but you knew she was lying. I mean—really, Mom? *Of course* everyone would notice. Even worse, the only thing anyone would think about all day would be that enormous, disgusting, hideous growth on your face. And that's exactly how it played out. Right?

Okay, maybe someone did notice. And maybe someone did make a comment (I hope not, but, hey, kids can be cruel). But I can *absolutely guarantee* that your pimple was not the primary thing on anyone else's mind that day. I would make any bet you wanted about this—that's how sure I am. The day you had that life-altering pimple was the day that *every other person was worrying about themselves.* In other words, it was just like every other day. Your mother was right (or at least mostly right). No matter how the situation looked to you that day, everyone else was too busy with their own stuff to give you as much grief about that pimple as you were expecting. Even if (especially if) someone made a nasty comment to you.

When someone does something mean or crappy to you, *it's about them, not about you.* It's an expression of their own insecurity or unhappiness or whatever else is going on inside them. That's how humans work. We act based on our own internal thoughts and perceptions. We don't have a clue what's going on inside someone else, most of the time, because we're so caught up in our own views of circumstances. The snotty clerk at the perfume counter who ignored you for over ten minutes? In her head, she was busy trying to figure out how she could make dinner and get her child to band practice even though her other child had to get new cleats for soccer before the game that night. She wasn't ignoring you because you weren't dressed well enough, or didn't have perfect hair. She was caught up in her own perspective of what was going on, and *it was not about you.* Or let's imagine for a moment that she did see you, and she wasn't trying to mentally multi-task, and she didn't like what you were wearing, or didn't think you were going to make a purchase. Those thoughts, those perspectives, were *not about you.* Those thoughts—and her action of not waiting on you for over ten minutes—were about her, and *only* her. They were based on *her perceptions*, not on *your reality*.

Since you have the awesome power to create your own thoughts, feelings, and actions, no one else can do it for you, and what you come up with is the sole responsibility of—you. If you are feeling hurt or offended or not good enough—well, that's up to you. Another person may take an action or say something that you don't agree with, but how it *affects* you and whether you internalize that their attitude as meaning something about you, is entirely up to you.

You can learn to recognize and accept what is difficult, without losing sight of your ability to create your own reality. It's based on the idea that while pain is real, suffering is optional. This isn't about pretending something painful hasn't happened. It's about choosing how you respond and how you frame your own reality.

There's a pose in yoga called Pigeon Pose. It can be done lying face down or on your back or in a chair (all are different modifications of the same basic pose). It's what is known as a hip-opener—a pose that's meant to stretch the muscles around your hip bones, the ones that get really tight from too much sitting. Interestingly, yoga teachers frequently make the comment that "emotions are stored in the hips," which means that hip-opener poses are often very uncomfortable to do, and that working on this can unleash a flood of (unexpected) emotion when the tension is released.

Why does this matter? Because practicing Pigeon Pose is one of the best ways to learn the difference between pain and suffering. It's a way to really experience this difference in your body, so you can translate that learning for your brain. When you are in Pigeon Pose, your body starts to experience discomfort—a *lot* of discomfort (unless you are über-flexible; even so, at some point you had to go through discomfort to get that flexible). As soon as your body begins to feel discomfort, what do you think it does? It tightens up. You begin to tense your muscles, sometimes even before you have actually felt the pain, in *anticipation of the pain*. Yes, it does hurt. The pain is real. However, the story you start to create about the pain, the perspective that you take on the pain, determines whether you start to suffer.

When your muscles are tense and you're trying to avoid pain, you are far more acutely conscious of the pain. You are fighting against it (it's an instinctive response) and that starts those fire alarms going off in your head. You already know where that leads: noise, confusion, suffering. However, if you take action to breathe into the pain (again with the breathing), your muscles start to relax, the alarms in your head quiet down, and it doesn't feel quite as bad. There's still discomfort (that's the reality piece), but the *suffering* isn't amping up the volume, so it's a lot more tolerable. Your muscles start to relax when you're not tensing them up in anticipation of going into fight-flight-or-freeze mode.

Your brain takes a lot of cues from your body. When you are able to calm your body to some degree, your brain starts to calm down. Your internal screen goes from high-definition to regular viewing, and you have the opportunity to assess the situation and choose your perspective. Pretty cool, huh?

Try This

Let's start with the seated Pigeon Pose (unless you are already familiar with Pigeon Pose, in which case do whatever version will get you a discomfort vs. suffering result). Sit upright in a chair. Take your right ankle and lay it across your left knee. Try to get your right leg to be parallel with the floor (the tighter you are, the harder that will be; don't worry about it). When your right ankle is over your left knee, sit up nice and tall, and then bend forward towards the floor with a straight back. Don't curve your back—keep it straight and bend forward from your hips. Very soon you will feel a sense of pulling and discomfort in your right hip area. Notice the discomfort and notice your automatic reaction to pull away and release the pose. Now take a couple of those four-count breaths we talked about earlier. As you exhale on the second round, slowly allow yourself to bend a little further (still with a straight back). Notice the area of discomfort and any differences from when you first tried to bend forward, before you did the magic breathing. If you have let yourself breathe, your muscles have relaxed, even if it's only a tiny bit, and the pose has become a little less uncomfortable than before. This is how you begin to transform from suffering to pain—by loosening up a little and allowing it. (Do the same with your left leg, to balance your body.)

Keys to Happiness

There's a lot written on the secret to happiness. The funny thing is, it's not really a secret. Even though the answer is pretty simplistic and basic, people keep writing about and searching for it, as if the information is hidden away somehow. It's not. Here it is: *The secret to happiness is having self-compassion, gratitude,* and *perspective.* That's it. Now you have the key to being happy. That doesn't seem so hard, right? Did it work yet?

Self-compassion is a combination of self-kindness, mindfulness, and an understanding of common humanity—the ways your experiences are similar to those of all people's. When you treat yourself well, with care and kindness, you are better able to understand that "this too shall pass," and you are not permanently doomed to misery. You are able to get a sense of perspective (that *meta view*) and begin to see that there's a light in the darkness.

Self-compassion is what wearing rose-colored glasses is all about. It's a willingness to see your life as a work in progress, with natural ups and downs. It's about making the choice to *focus on what is possible*, rather than focusing on *what won't work.* So, just as you choose what to wear or what to eat, you can choose how you view the world, what perspective to take. You can choose the lens through which you see yourself and your life. By making the choice to see your life through a lens of self-compassion, you support yourself on the path to happiness.

But don't leave out the gratitude. That's like leaving the yeast out when you're making bread. You'll still get something edible, but it won't be nearly as enjoyable. Gratitude is the glue that holds together self-compassion and perspective. It's what allows you to recognize that you have had some positive experiences in your life, even though they might be hard to remember in this particular moment. The field of Positive Psychology has given us a lot of research in the area of gratitude. An ongoing practice of gratitude is the one thing, above all others, that *improved and maintained* people's sense of being happier. Seriously.

There is a trick to practicing gratitude. It's that you have to actually *feel* grateful. Just saying, "I'm grateful for..." blah, blah, blah won't do anything except annoy you. Experiencing gratitude isn't about making a superficial list of things you think you *should* be grateful for. It's about taking a moment to feel the internal sensation of truly being grateful for something. It doesn't have to be profound or complicated, this thing you're genuinely grateful for.

We often think of things in the abstract, and say we're grateful or thankful. How many times have you heard someone say, "I'm grateful for my health" or "I'm grateful I have a roof over my head"—and even though you hear them saying the words, you don't really have a sense that they are *experiencing* gratitude. It's more like lip service to gratitude while, inside, they're really thinking how unhappy they are about something else. Compare that to a person who has recovered from a difficult illness and who says, "I'm grateful for my health." You can hear the ring of conviction in what they say. In that moment, you have no doubt the person is experiencing the sensation of gratitude. You can see it on their face.

Try This

Think of something you are grateful for. Something real. Maybe it's a beautiful sunset. Maybe it's getting a hug right when you needed it. Maybe it's the feeling of your dog cuddling close when you weren't feeling well. Bring up that memory with as many senses involved as you can. Feel it, taste it, smell it, see it. *Now* acknowledge your feeling of gratitude. Pay attention to what this feels like in your body. (Maybe even notice your shoulders—they might have relaxed a little.)

Let's get perspective involved in being happy. Be courageous. Think of a situation that got your heart rate going and caused your forehead to wrinkle. Really get into that moment of frustration and irritation. Notice how your body is reacting (because you can't practice that too much). Are you all worked up? Now finish this sentence, from your heart: *This* is *good, because...*" Take a stand by challenging yourself to actively answer with a *truth*. You'll likely struggle with this, and that's fine. The automatic denial or a "No, it really *isn't* good" is the measure of how entrenched you are in your current perspective. If happiness is a choice, you can *find the good*. It's there, right alongside the frustrating, the upsetting, and the bad.

Motivation

Happiness through perspective (and self-compassion and gratitude) makes sense—but how do you get motivated to start implementing these ideas? Sometimes motivation comes from *disliking* something, like having a messy house when the in-laws come to visit, which motivates you to clean up in order to avoid those negative looks; or finishing that report for your boss, so you won't "get in trouble." There's a more positive, productive alternative available, though.

Whatever the task is, *start it*. You don't even have to be motivated to *begin taking action*. Action requires a commitment to *doing*, which is a straightforward cognitive process. Here's how to go about it: Raise your left arm, and then put it down. You didn't have to delve deeply into your motivational psyche to take that action. You read the words and did the action. (If you didn't, that's okay, too. You get the point.)

You can get so caught up in your thoughts—*I don't feel like it, I'm not in the mood, It's too hard*—that *you stop taking action*. It can be helpful to stand up for a minute, take a walk to the bathroom and back, and maybe take a few deep breaths. Those are all *actions,* and that little bit of movement can set you on track again with taking other actions.

If you wait until you feel like you are ready or have sufficient motivation, there's a good chance you won't get to it at all. Remember that book you dreamed of writing? The new style of cooking you were going to check out? That super cool project you keep meaning to start? You keep putting it off because the time isn't right, and so it doesn't happen. Here's your opportunity: act on it anyway. *Start.* As Lao-Tzu said, "The journey of a thousand miles starts with a single step." Go ahead and take that first one.

Try This

Set a timer and *do it* (whatever *it* is) for thirty minutes. Chances are, you will keep going even longer than you'd anticipated. That will jump start the project and you will likely feel fantastic that you've really done something about it. Feeling fantastic is a sure-fire motivation for doing more.

≫ ≪

You've reviewed a *lot* of information in this chapter, so you may want to come back and go over it again later. For the sake of simplicity (and if you're like me and want to keep going forward without pausing now), let's hit the high point of this chapter again: Happiness is achieved through *self-compassion, gratitude,* and *perspective.* Those are the basic ingredients for successfully managing anything life throws your way, whether it's an exciting, scary, or challenging thing. They allow your creativity to rise and shine (and be super yummy).

Now that you have a grounding in the basics, you're ready for the detailing. The next chapter addresses your own special sauce, the extra ingredients that help you *own your best self.*

Chapter 7
O—Own Your Best Self

"You yourself, as much as anybody in the entire universe, deserve your love and affection."
Buddha

Once upon a time, there was a young woman named Bethany. She had a loving family, a supportive boyfriend, and a job she adored. But she wasn't happy. She didn't like her body (she felt she needed to lose weight), she didn't like her appearance (she felt unattractive), and she didn't like her career (she felt that everyone else was doing more). Basically, she didn't like who she was, and that bothered her. A lot. Whenever anyone tried to help her see her strengths and the positives about herself, she would say, "I know who I am, but it's not who I want to be." She couldn't accept a compliment, even from her boyfriend. She knew that the proper way to receive a compliment was to say, "Thank you," but in her head (and, more often than not, out loud), she would instead say, "You're just saying that to try and make me feel better" or "You have to say that—you're my boyfriend" (or mother, sister, or friend). There was nothing Bethany saw about herself that was good enough. That made her very unhappy.

Bethany tried to get help. She read books, went to therapy, talked to friends. She meditated (or tried to), she got hypnotized. Nothing worked. She figured "not good enough" in every area would be the story of her life. She got so used to that way of thinking about herself that it became automatic. She would get a good review at work and think, *They're just being nice to me. I'm not as good as Sarah* (or whichever co-worker came to mind first). When her boyfriend would tell her she looked good, she would immediately list at least five things that were not good (from her perspective). When her parents told her they were proud of her, she would half-smile, but she would think, *My sisters really have their lives together. I'm just pathetic.*

And so it went, day after day. Bethany felt like she was sinking deeper and deeper into quicksand, with no escape. Wherever she looked, whatever she thought about, she saw more evidence of her failings. It was a banner day when she was able to assess her work performance as "adequate," although that thought was quickly followed by several thoughts about all the ways she needed to improve.

This is the point in the story where we usually expect the magical solution. The place for a fairy godmother or a lightning strike or winning the lottery. Something big; something dramatic. Because if this story keeps going in the same direction, it is going to be pretty depressing. I don't know about you, but I love happy endings. I love the point when the sun begins to peak out from behind the clouds, and you know there's going to be a rainbow soon. I love the moment of revelation that sparks a new beginning, even when the road is still going uphill. I love it when the light starts to be visible, indicating there is an end to the tunnel and an opportunity to move past the present circumstances. Bethany and I met at the point when she had stopped believing in rainbows. She was making a last-ditch effort to see if the rain would ever stop falling, or if she was going to drown as the river kept rising around her.

What Bethany hadn't realized yet, and the key to turning her story around, was that she was wrong. Totally, absolutely, completely wrong when she saw herself as "less than" anyone else. She was working on an incorrect assumption. She thought that her worth was *in comparison to* other people. Nope. Not at all. Her worth was all about her—and she was worthy because she was a living, breathing, human being. She was worthy as a living breathing *being*—the human part was optional.

Bethany hadn't been giving herself love or affection. She was missing the point of the Buddha quote that starts this chapter: "You yourself, as much as anybody in the entire universe, deserve your love and affection." Bethany was no better, *and no worse*, than anyone else in the universe. Because had not been giving herself her own love and affection, she couldn't accept the love and affection of anyone else. Bethany had fallen into the trap of believing that there was some kind of "goodness hierarchy" in the universe, and that she was at the bottom of it. Since she didn't believe she measured up to how she saw other people, she figured she was out of luck. She couldn't have been more wrong.

After I listened to Bethany's story, I asked her this question: "Do you have—or have you ever had—a best friend?" Her gaze was puzzled as she affirmed that yes, she had a best friend. I asked her, "How do you talk to your best friend?" With an even more confused gaze, she said she didn't know what I was asking. Here's how our conversation went:

Me: "If your best friend said that she's was not good enough, that nothing she did was worth anything, that she was unskilled, untalented, and unattractive, what would you say to her?"

Bethany: "I would tell her that's not true at all! I would list for her all the things that are wonderful about her (and there are a lot). I would tell her I was sorry to hear she felt that way, but that she was absolutely wrong. I would say that she is wonderful, kind, caring, and beautiful, and that I love having her as a friend, because she brings so much joy to my life."

Me: "How would you feel if she told you that she appreciated your kindness, but she knew you were only saying that to make her feel better?"

Bethany: "I would be pretty mad. And frustrated. I would tell her that she was out of her mind, and that anyone could see how awesome she was."

Me: "Would you yell at her or speak to her with compassion, even if your heart was breaking, as she told you how she felt?"

Bethany: "Of course I wouldn't yell at her. I would do anything to convince her, to show her, how wonderful she is."

Me: "So what would happen if you treated yourself with the same love, compassion, and understanding that you treat your best friend?"

I'm not a fairy godmother (although that would be super cool), and I'm not suggesting this conversation was the equivalent of a lightning strike… except it was. Bethany looked at me, looked away, and then looked back at me. She started to speak, stopped, then took a deep breath and said, "I don't know. I've never done that. I see everything that I don't like, and even if I think something went okay, I can always see all the ways it could have been better."

Bethany was on the edge of a *really* big revelation. One that would change everything. Maybe you've skirted close to that edge, and then backed away. A lot of people get *so close*, and then convince themselves that they should stick with what they know—or think they know—which is that they don't measure up, and that it's not going to change.

After all the work she had done in getting to me, Bethany was ready. She was ready to step into a different way of viewing herself, and so she did. It wasn't magic dust that made it happen. She was simply and finally ready to imagine a new perspective. She was ready to learn the truth of the words of Oscar Wilde: "To love oneself is the beginning of a life-long romance." She was ready to understand that if she could be a best friend to someone else (and she was), then she was also capable of being a best friend to the most important person in the world to her—*herself.*

Perhaps you've developed your own version of Bethany's story. Maybe you have a deep-down sense that you *aren't good enough.* You might have been told this by someone important when you were a child. You might have figured it out for yourself when life didn't work out the way you hoped. You might suspect that it's true. It's the secret you don't want to admit to anyone—least of all yourself. It's the stuff of nightmares, insomnia, anxiety, depression, and *stress.*

Or maybe you've spent years trying to convince yourself and the world that it's not true, that you *are* good enough. This might have resulted in you working more than anyone around you. It might have shown itself in you feeling *hugely* defensive if someone at work suggests that they want to add something *in addition* to what you've already proposed. It might mean that you don't know how to set reasonable limits and boundaries for yourself, and so you volunteer to do anything and everything, because it's "the right thing to do." Perhaps you feel like a *total failure* if you miss one day at the gym, or one of your kid's basketball games, or if you don't volunteer to be a room mother enough times during the year. Whatever your standard of measurement is, you continuously seek data to reinforce your belief that you have to *do more, be more, and achieve more,* because you aren't enough just as you are.

Although Bethany excelled at compassion for other people (she even worked with young children with behavioral problems), she had a different standard for herself. She believed that she needed to be perfect, and that she *had* to keep trying, and beating herself up, until she attained that state. The biggest truth Bethany was missing was that *we are all perfectly imperfect, just as we are.* This includes you.

If you have ever had a moment when you know, to the very core, that you are not good enough, then you are struggling in the same quicksand as Bethany. In quicksand, the more you struggle, the further down you sink. The key to surviving quicksand is to remain calm, not struggle, and try to lie on your back and float, or do a backstroke to safety. Patience, the physical form of compassion, is the most important action to take when in quicksand. Accepting that you are in a tough situation, letting go of panic, and trying to float is what helps you get to solid ground.

You can follow that same pattern whenever you are starting to (internally) thrash around and fight (or succumb) to the mind-suck of self-doubt and negativity. Take a breath. Slow down. Recognize that you need to implement the float technique of compassion, which means accepting the feelings you're having with love and caring. Remind yourself that you are imperfect (just like everyone else), and that, if you treat yourself as your own best friend, you are going to survive and make it back to solid ground.

When your best friend is struggling and having a hard time or getting down on herself, you listen. You empathize with her feelings. You remind her of all that is phenomenal, wonderful, and amazing about her. You might even make a few comparisons—but they'll all involve your friend as the heroine. You are her cheerleader, confidante, and defender. You might acknowledge the grain of truth in what she's saying ("Yeah, sometimes you do get really cranky and make impulsive decisions), but you do it in a way that validates her worth and normalizes her behavior ("But everyone does that"). You remind her that even if she has handled something in a manner that's less than perfect, that's okay ("You screwed up. So what? Remember when you told me last month how your boss lost the company $20,000? Crap happens. At least you caught your mistake right away, so no one lost any money. And now you know how to do it better the next time"). You are caring, patient, and *kind* with your friend. You allow her to *own* her behavior and you do your best to put her behavior in perspective, while keeping sight of her inner goodness. You are her best friend, *and you act that way.*

Compare that to how you treat yourself, especially in moments when you are feeling you aren't good enough. You are probably demanding, critical, maybe even cruel. You speak harshly to yourself, and you don't tolerate even minor transgressions. Everything is evidence of what is *wrong* about you. Whatever the standard, you don't meet it. And if, by some miracle, you recognize a strength in yourself, you quickly revert to the *much* longer list of your failings. It doesn't matter that no one else sees those as failings. You know the truth, sad and disheartening as it is. Except there's a flaw in your reasoning.

You aren't treating yourself the way you would treat someone you care about. You are focusing on, and emphasizing, only a *part* of the story. Even when you tell yourself you're being objective, you're not. You are so busy trying not to fool yourself into thinking too well of yourself (like that's going to really happen), you're missing out on the rest of the story. It absolutely makes sense to acknowledge when something has gone wrong, or is late, or doesn't match a set of pre-determined external expectations. *But that doesn't happen in a vacuum.* If you are assessing your failings (I love the word fail, because if you failed, you tried), you're probably not seeing it that way. If you view the "failure" as evidence that you are engaged and working to learn and move forward, then "failure" is not the accurate word to use. You can choose to assess your successes and strengths, as well. And you can choose to do that in a caring, compassionate, and kind manner. Because you would *never, ever* speak to your best friend the way you have been speaking to yourself.

Here's a way for you to try this. Imagine that you are a princess. Not the kind of princess who is just arm candy, or who doesn't get to make her own decisions. Not a Disney please-rescue-me kind of princess. Imagine you are a Xena Warrior princess-type: strong, independent, intelligent, empowered, with a positive sense of self, who values who you are and who chooses friends and companions wisely. *Someone who doesn't feel she has to settle, and who sees herself as good enough.* This princess stands tall in her self-worth. She has the self-perception and confidence to realize she is a person of worth and value, *just as she is.* She is a woman in charge of her own destiny.

Try This

Sit up tall. Even taller. Move your shoulders back. How do you feel? When you sit up straight with shoulders back, do you feel a little better? Stronger, or more positive? Slouching or bending in on yourself works against self-esteem. Picture a person sitting next to you on the bus, at work, or at dinner in a restaurant who is sitting up with good posture. We are drawn to people with good posture. We notice the person who is sitting tall. They seem confident, self-assured, and able to command respect, even from strangers. Compare that to the person who sits slouched in a chair with their shoulders forward, head down. They're giving the impression that something is wrong, that they're not so competent or capable, and perhaps even are not good enough.

Now imagine you are a warrior princess and you are in a public venue. There are many people around you, and all of them want to get to know you. What do you do? Do you accept every invitation? Really? You're going to accept every invitation that comes your way, from this entire crowd?

Absolutely not. No matter how nice, kind, and interested you are, you will be careful and discriminating in your choices. *This is a good thing.* The ability to differentiate, to determine what meets your needs, and to make decisions that take them into consideration is a skill. The warrior princess doesn't accept every invitation to engage.

If the person asking is unkind, unfair, unruly, unhappy; if they don't have something positive and unique to recommend them, then it's not happening. This warrior princess knows her worth. She doesn't doubt that she's good enough, so she is able to accurately assess what is in her own best interest, and in the interests of the people and beliefs she cares about.

As you look around at the many people vying for your time and attention, you will single out those people who appear the most positive. Depending on your own criteria, the characteristics you look for may be humor, intelligence, caring, a strong work ethic, or any of countless other factors. Our own definitions of what we consider to be positive, guides our choices. You are not compelled to accept someone, or their beliefs or choices, simply because they ask you. Certainly, if you are a princess, you will rule out anyone who falls below your personal criteria for engagement. This makes good sense. There are so many potential people to connect with, so many options. *You do not need to be led by scarcity.* There are enough possibilities.

Imagine using the Warrior Princess Principle in all areas of your life. *You treat yourself well, value who you are, value your own time, attention, and level of involvement, and trust that there are possibilities.*

You understand, accept, and utilize your ability to say no—to people who don't see your value, to people who take and don't give, to people who would not treat you well, and to treating yourself poorly because you were momentarily caught in quicksand. You, know you have the means and the ability to get yourself out.

You also understand, accept, and utilize the ability to say yes—to happiness, to seeing your own worth, to being treated well, to living your full potential, to treating yourself with caring, kindness, and compassion. You say yes to being your own best friend, and that enhances all your other relationships. You say yes to knowing you are awesome, just as you are.

Bethany started with learning to be her own best friend. She realized that her self-talk was usually very cruel, and that if she ever talked that way to a friend, the relationship would probably end very quickly. She began to practice accepting compliments from people she knew really loved her. She was able to start doing that because she realized that every time she rejected their positive words, she was giving them a message of "You're lying" or "I can't trust you to be honest." She did trust her family, friends, and boyfriend. A major impact for Bethany was when she asked each of them (in a sort of a mini poll) what it was like for them when she brushed off their compliments or praise. She was surprised to discover how hurt and frustrated they felt by it.

After a few weeks of treating herself as a valued friend, Bethany began to notice a difference. There were fewer times when she felt absolutely horrible about herself—and many times when she felt good enough. Bethany also used the Warrior Princess Principle, with a focus on sitting and standing tall. She was amazed at the difference that small change made, and found that it reinforced her positive inner dialogue. That led to even more changes. She started attending a yoga class, didn't worry as much about her grades (she was finishing a degree), and noticed that she had a lot more energy and enthusiasm for her daily life.

If you haven't been your own best friend, now is a *great* time to start. I use the hashtag #ownbestfriend in all my social media, as a reminder to myself, and to spread the word. Jump on this bandwagon with me.

>>> <<<

In these first few chapters we've covered how you can enhance your energy, make more time, and practice perspective (along with self-compassion and gratitude). Now, with this chapter, we've covered being your own best friend. But wait—there's more. Next up, you're going to Wake Up Your Inner Rock Star and stand even taller.

Chapter 8
W—Wake Up Your Inner Rock Star

I discovered my inner rock star in a totally random moment. I was in a gift shop and started trying on goofy hats. I couldn't stop laughing at the ridiculous picture I made wearing a cow hat and then a leopard hat. My husband said, "Quiet down. People are watching you," and that's when it hit me. That's when the huge, momentous, absolutely life-changing magic of waking up my inner rock star hit me full in the face: *I didn't care.* Yup, people were watching. Probably some of them were amused, and possibly some of them were annoyed. I wasn't trying to be a spectacle, but I was laughing uncontrollably and looking foolish. *And it just didn't matter.* I was having a blast. I was totally in the moment and enjoying myself. So why was me doing that such a big deal?

Like many people, I had spent a lot of time worried about what other people thought. I wanted people to like me. I was often self-conscious on the inside but trying to look comfortable and composed on the outside. I cared about other people's opinions, sometimes to the point of not making choices to get what I wanted. I generally appeared self-confident and self-assured. But not on the inside. I worried about whether I looked good enough, how what I said would be received, and whether I was doing the "right" thing. I never wanted to look foolish, or to be seen as inappropriate. I wanted people to think well of me. *Regardless of what I really wanted.* That yellow car is the perfect example.

In my 30s I fell in love with a sunny, bright yellow car. I debated buying it. I talked to (almost) everyone and got a lot of feedback. Mostly, people said something like, "You want a what? Yellow? Really?" Sometimes people laughed or look perplexed. Someone may have said, "Go for it," but if so, I don't remember. What I *do* remember is doubting myself and my decision, not being sure if it really was a good idea. I didn't get the car.

Buying or not buying a car isn't the biggest deal in the world. It's not going to affect you for the rest of your life, right? Well, maybe that's true for some people. I kept thinking about that yellow car. Every time I saw one, I felt a pang of wistfulness and regret. I would remind myself that I'd made the sensible decision. That it hadn't been a good idea to get that car. I'd add in any other justification I could come up with for not following my own heart. That went on for years. I could have purchased a yellow car, but something inside me wouldn't and couldn't stomach going against the grain of other people's opinions. I'd recall the looks, the reactions people had when I'd talked with them about getting that car, and then I'd push the desire away again. I was so far from my true self in those moments. If I had an inner rock star, she was clearly off doing something else.

I hadn't yet discovered that famous, fantastic Marianne Williamson quote: "Our deepest fear is not that we are inadequate. Our deepest fear is that we are powerful beyond measure. It is our light, not our darkness that most frightens us." Truthfully, if I had seen that quote, I wouldn't have believed it. It wouldn't have resonated with me, because I had done such a good job of convincing myself that I had already dealt with "all that stuff," and any self-doubt was really a realistic assessment. Have you been there? To that place where you are miles and miles away from being able to see your greatness because you have totally, completely convinced yourself that you *are* being objective, and you *just don't measure up*?

I have met so many women (and men) who carry a deeply rooted belief of "I am not good enough." Sometimes it's near the surface and a part of conscious thought. More often, it's a hidden shadow that peeks out at the first sight of any possible vulnerability, whispering messages of doubt and denigration. It's the voice of the inner critic (who isn't really you, but *seems* to be), listing all of the "nots"—cannot, should not, *better not*. It's the multiplied echo of anytime anyone said something cruel, thoughtless, or unkind to you. It's the reflection of past mistakes, large or small, distorted in the funhouse mirror, so they appear overwhelming and overpowering.

And yet, the most important *fact* is the one that's hardest to see: *It's all crap*. Those inner messages, thoughts, perceptions, and beliefs are *false*. There is only one real truth: You are *more* than good enough, just as you are. No, you're not perfect (and no one ever has been or ever will be perfect). You are human. This means you are a learning, growing, evolving being. Your perfection is in your imperfection. Your inner possibilities are endless. Truth.

Don't believe me? Consider the brain. What do you know of how the brain works? We, as a society, have very little knowledge of the full capacity of the brain. The one thing we can be sure of is that there's so much about it that we don't know. We have ideas, theories, and beliefs, but not comprehensive *knowing*. The greatest thinkers and scientists of all time, have not, and do not, have this answer. Because we are *all* still evolving. Maybe, someday, someone will know everything about how the human brain works. That day is not today. The more we learn about it, the more we realize how much we have to learn. The only thing we can be absolutely certain of is that we are imperfect. Hallelujah. You are in the company of all of humankind.

The Four Agreements

Are you familiar with the works of Don Miguel Ruiz? He has written many books full of ancient Toltec wisdom. The basis of his work is the Four Agreements. They are a way of understanding who we really are, accepting who we are, and celebrating who we are and our place in this world. It's a roadmap for how to live your life, as your phenomenal, amazing, flawed, perfectly imperfect, rock star self. These are the Four Agreements:

1. Be impeccable with your word.
2. Don't take anything personally.
3. Don't make assumptions.
4. Always do your best.

Following these Four Agreements opens a whole new vista of potential, a doorway into connecting with your true self. It is a guided path to seeing yourself (and everyone else) as good enough. For me, using the Four Agreements was the first step in being able to consider the idea of being "powerful beyond measure." The magical key was understanding that everything I do, think, feel, and perceive is based on *my own perspective*—just like everyone else is thinking, feeling, perceiving, and acting from their own perspective (which is why you don't have to take anything personally). This isn't permission to act in a less-than-kind way towards someone else, because if you are following all four of the agreements, you are always doing your best, and you are not making assumptions. Pretty cool, huh?

When you begin to internalize the idea that *you* are responsible for your own thoughts, feelings, and actions, and you are not responsible for anyone else's thoughts, feelings, or actions, it opens a doorway to finding your own voice. This is your chance to speak up for yourself and start to live your truth. Adam Galinsky has a great TED Talk about this. He talks about our perceptions of the "range of acceptable behavior," which underlies and reinforces our sense of our power. There's a double bind that many of us have developed. We have had the experience of not speaking up, and going unnoticed. And we have also had the experience of speaking up and being punished with some sort of negative response. This double bind creates (and limits) what we believe is our range of acceptable behavior. Here's the awesome news, though: When you stretch that range, utilizing the core beliefs behind the four agreements, you begin to redefine for yourself what is acceptable. You start to realize that everyone else is reacting from *their own perspectives*, and since that's not about you… you can begin to really own what you know and who you are.

Strengths

If you are like so many of the people I have worked with, the first task toward becoming a rock star is identifying your strengths. This is a way to start shifting you view of yourself. You can create a super long list of what you wish was different, but your list of personal strengths is often a lot shorter. This doesn't mean you are lacking in any way—it just means that you aren't giving yourself credit for the truly amazing person you are. So it's time to rethink that perspective and start connecting to the basics of your rock star self.

It can be really daunting to develop a list of your strengths, especially if you already have decided that there are only about five or six of them (you know because you've tried an exercise like this before). Here's the good news: There's a great research-based tool that can help you do this.

It's called the Values in Action survey, and it's based in the science of Positive Psychology. It was created exactly for the purpose of helping people identify their strengths.

Try This
Take the Values in Action (VIA) survey to identify your 24 character strengths. Everyone has 24 strengths listed in their results. The survey is to figure out their prioritized order and to identify your top five "signature strengths." You can find and take the free survey online at www.viacharacter.org. There's great information available throughout the site, including blog posts like "24 Ways to Put Your Strengths to Work." You can also save your results (just remember your login information) and retake the survey again later to see if your strengths have shifted.

After you've taken the survey, you will have a list of 24 character strengths to build from. Even better, you can work to focus on particular strengths, if you want to increase a specific area. Since the brain has neuroplasticity (this is one of the things we *do* know about the brain), which is the ability to create new neural pathways, and that allows you to develop (and enjoy) new behaviors. You have the ability to create the totally rock star "you" that you'd like to be.

Roles

The second area that is vitally important for truly being "you" is to assess the roles that you take in your life. Are you the peacemaker? The caretaker? The provider? The rescuer? The superstar? You might be the advocate, the consultant, the friend, or the fixer. Perhaps you have the role of family transporter (free taxi service), gift-buyer, cleaner (doing all the cleaning or taking charge of making sure it gets done). You may be a spouse, partner, parent, child, sibling, and/or grandparent. Or a community leader, an organizer, the "willing hands" that always volunteer; a conversation starter or the quiet one in the room; the moral guide or the disillusioned citizen. There are countless roles people play, and each of us has at least a handful going on at any given moment. Your roles also change over the course of your life and across different situations.

When you begin to define the roles that are currently part of your life, you are open to deciding which roles you want. Yes, *want*. When I mentioned roles you may have immediately started thinking in terms of obligation and responsibility. Take a deep breath. Take another breath (don't hyperventilate). This is a really big step. This is about ownership of *who you really want to be*. Do your very best to stay out of the trap of "this won't work because...." Treat yourself kindly, with compassion, and with a sense of interest and exploration. You are investigating—assessing and weighing *how* you want to be in your life.

Try This

Take a look at the roles you can identify in your life at this moment (you can always come back and look at the past, but for right now, stay focused on the present). Pour a cup of coffee, and sit down for a brainstorming session to create a list for yourself of as many roles you have as you can define. If you get stuck, try thinking about someone else and how you would describe the roles they play in their life, and then see if that triggers additional role descriptors for yourself.

The purpose of this exercise is to recognize the ways in which the roles you take in life have defined your sense of self. Because, even if you don't believe it, you have choice in whether or not you continue in those roles. (Yes, even if you are a parent. You can choose the good parent role or the overinvolved parent role, or the parent-as-friend role. You can be the limit-setter or the soother. It's an endless list of possibilities.)

Go back through the list of roles you made and decide which ones you want to have going forward. It may take a few tries for you to complete this. I strongly suggest that you do this exercise at least a couple of times, over the span of a few days. Give yourself time to ponder, to truly consider what you want in your life. Instead of spending time detailing how you "can't" change, hold off on implementation of shifting your roles until you have decided *what you want*.

The final step in this process is to ask yourself this question: *How can I make this happen?* That's it. That's the central question that determines the success of your newly found role definition. It's a "how" question. It is not *Why won't this work?* or *What's wrong with choosing this role?* or any version of *I can't*. Your question (your mission, should you choose to accept it) is to decide what you need to do in order to implement the roles you want, and let go of the ones that are not serving you well.

Remember my story of trying on silly hats in the store and people noticing? While tears of laughter were running down my cheeks and I was bent over from laughing so hard, I had that amazing revelation about being a rock star that changed my life. I discovered that it didn't matter what someone else thought of me, and that was the start of the journey to truly being myself. I began to assess and let go of roles that no longer fit the me I wanted to be. I started to do things I hadn't done or wouldn't have done before. I started really *doing yoga*. Meaning I stopped looking at other people and hoping I was doing the poses "right." I began to laugh when I would fall and land in a heap on the floor. I began to take more chances and do more silly things. I went to Disney World with my family and wore a tiara *all day long*. (I thought it was really pretty. I totally mortified my teenage daughter). I started shamanic training, because I didn't care if it seemed "too weird; too woo-woo," because it fascinated me. I said yes to things I loved, and no to things that felt too much like obligations. I changed jobs so I could have more time to do what I love (that was *huge*.).

And then I bought a sunny, bright yellow car. I am absolutely, totally, completely in love with my yellow car. I remember what everyone said eighteen years ago. *It just doesn't matter*. Every time I look at my yellow car, I smile. I smile because it's so cheery, so sunny, and it makes me so happy. But, most of all, I smile because buying that car was my choice, and *I listened to myself*. I smile because this is my life, and I am *living* it—without worrying about someone else's opinion; without worrying about my worth as a person.

I do feel like a rock star when I drive my yellow car, because I feel totally and completely *myself*. That's my definition of a rock star: someone who is willing to be truly, authentically themselves, without worry about what other people think; someone who embraces happiness and joy in their life; someone who has chosen who and how they want to be in the world, and puts that into practice. You don't have to buy a yellow car to find and honor your true self, which probably involves something entirely different for you. But, whatever it is, *do it*. Take the risk. Go on the trip, dance in the rain, wear the tiara. Don't worry about what other people are thinking—do what you desire to do, and let your heart sing. Laugh out loud, act silly, and enjoy each moment of your precious life. Know that you are absolutely perfect just as you are, and celebrate your perfect imperfection. Listen to your inner voice and be true to yourself. You don't have to worry about anyone's opinion—*honor your own*.

Are you feeling pumped up by realizing that *you* get to decide whether you wear a cape and tights or wear white after Labor Day (does anyone follow that old fashion rule anymore?)? If you think back to a time you dressed up in something beautiful or wore an awesome costume for a party, that's the feeling you're going for—just by being *you*.

Importantly, in this chapter you've moved into a place of freedom and flow. That's right where you need to be in order to take the next step. In the next chapter, you'll Envision Your Inner Purpose. And yes, you do have one (or more), even if you've felt it's been missing your whole life.

Chapter 9
E—Envision Your Inner Purpose

*"What is the soul? Consciousness. The more
awareness, the deeper the soul, and when such
essence overflows, you feel a sacredness around."*
Rumi, The Soul of Rumi

I feel like something is missing in my life. I know there must be more. I need to discover my inner purpose." That was Sandi when I met her. I introduced her to you in Chapter 1. She was a bright, articulate, caring, and compassionate woman who kept giving to everyone else in her life, while slipping deeper and deeper into feelings of self-doubt and hopelessness, interspersed by brief periods where she felt better. Sandi used to feel accomplished and positive, in touch with herself, her spirituality, and her dual careers of work and motherhood. Over time, life happened and she lost the connection to who she really was. One of the first things she told me was, "I want to get back my true self and find my inner purpose for this lifetime." She was coming up on a milestone birthday and that had accelerated her feelings of missing out, as well as increasing her sense of not being in touch with her true self.

As we began to work together, it became very clear to me that Sandi didn't see or value the tremendous gifts she had. Any time she inched toward seeing herself as positive or accomplished, she immediately shifted to a long recitation of all that she wasn't. She resisted to accepting herself as being good enough, and connected that to experiences from her childhood. That level of awareness was enhanced by her continual quest to find "the answer" through various books, podcasts, and programs.

In many aspects, our work together started off the same way. Sandi was eager to get to the root of her stuck place, and she wholeheartedly embraced any suggestions I gave for homework or practice—but only for a short time. She would start to make the tiniest bit of progress in self-acceptance and self-compassion, and then something external would occur and she'd be almost back to where she'd started (*almost*, because usually she'd gotten to a place that was a step or two *behind* where she'd been at first). Instead of slowly moving forward with small steps, she was a master of "one step forward, two steps backward."

Since that pattern came up so quickly, we were able to identify it. By working through the early steps of the EMPOWERS process, she made fantastic gains in learning to see and value herself more realistically. Like so many others, she developed a healthier personal routine, which included rest, exercise, a more reasonable work schedule, and increased time with her daughters. She gained confidence in her position at work, and embraced a promotion that previously would have left her feeling vulnerable and less important (being needed had been a trigger for her). Taking more of a management role initially brought the sense of being less involved, and therefore less valued and vital to her company—a stance consistent with her pattern of looking out for others and not herself. She saw that and solidified her practices of mindfulness, self-encouragement, and self-acceptance. She loved the successes she experienced, but the fly in the ointment remained that she hadn't found her inner purpose.

Inner Purpose

What's an inner purpose, anyway? (I use the words *soul purpose* and *inner purpose* interchangeably; use the one that fits best for you.) Over the last decade there's been a rise in alternative and complementary medicine in Western mainstream life. Practices such as meditation, yoga, reiki, pranayama (breathing techniques), and energy medicine (Emotional Freedom Technique or tapping, Eye Movement Desensitization and Reprocessing or EMDR) have gained popularity and acceptance. Being spiritual doesn't necessarily define someone as being weird or a hippie. All of these changes have led to a greater dialogue about finding and living one's inner purpose. That's fantastic, unless you end up feeling like you're the only one not on board. If the inner purpose train is leaving the station and you're still standing on the platform trying to find your ticket, what then? Or maybe you don't have an inner purpose at all, and that's why you can't find it? Even worse, what if you had it and lost it? Can inner purpose be recovered? Can it be re-found?

It helps to start with a definition. The Merriam-Webster Dictionary defines *soul* as "the immaterial essence, animating principle, or actuating cause of an individual life." *Purpose* is defined as "something set up as an object or end to be attained." Putting those together, I define *soul purpose* as "the journey to awareness of one's *animating principle* (the inner joy that sets you on fire) and the real-life implementation and *attainment* of whatever brings that joy." In other words, living your soul purpose means living a life that involves *doing the things that light you up*. The things that fascinate you, satisfy you, inspire you, bring you comfort; the things you do with such passion that you lose track of time; the things you *love to do*, whatever they are.

An inner purpose doesn't have to be a job (very often, it's not) or some big, grand mission. But it is something that you are *called* to do. *Called* in the sense that it happens with ease, that you could do it for hours, that it engages you from the inside out. *Called* in that your life wouldn't be as happy, bright, or interesting without it. Because you are called to live this soul purpose, you enhance the whole world. If you don't allow your soul purpose expression, you are depriving the universe of the special spark of magic is that is uniquely yours to share.

Here's the thing, though—your inner purpose isn't hiding under a rock somewhere. It's not passively sitting around waiting to be found (and it's not lost). At some level, you know your inner purpose, because you have experienced it at some point in your life. You might have only noticed the tip of your inner purpose iceberg, but it's inside you. Your inner purpose reflects your inner dreams and desires. Connecting with your inner purpose is about developing the *awareness* of your passions, and choosing to thrive, rather than merely existing and surviving. When you are connected to and living your inner purpose, you feel completely alive, unstoppable, and creative. In those moments, there are no limits— you are totally in alignment and in flow with the universe.

So how do you identify your inner purpose? It's easier than you may think. Start with thinking about what would be on your bucket list. What would you like to try doing, and what would you regret *not* having done? I love Kris Allen's song "Live Like You're Dying," because it's a reminder to be present in each moment. I don't really want to think about dying (that's probably pretty universal), but I absolutely want to have a life that I have *lived*.

We've already talked about choosing how you feel, and we talked about perspective (and ownership and self-compassion) as the key to being happy. Your inner purpose is about making the choice to live in a particular way, bringing in a sense of wonder and engagement. Many people think that an inner purpose is about providing some sort of service to others. You living your inner purpose—whatever it is—*is* a service to others. One of my favorite Rumi quotes says it all: "Spirit is so mixed with the visible world that giver, gift, and beneficiary are one thing. You are the grace raining down, the grace is you." You are the grace raining down, just by being you.

Jack Canfield, the author of *Chicken Soup for the Soul* and *The Success Principles*, believes that the real definition of success is fulfilling your inner purpose. He recommends two questions to help with coming to an awareness of inner purpose, that inner guiding light:

- "What are the two qualities that are most uniquely you?"
- "If the world were working perfectly, what would it look like according to you?"

These are great questions, and illustrate that each of us has our own vision of an ideal world, based on our own values, beliefs, strengths, and purpose. In the same way that your DNA or your fingerprint is uniquely yours, so is your inner purpose. It's about uncovering and then fanning the flame of your inner light, adding to the illumination of the world.

When I met with Karen, she made fast progress through the other steps of the EMPOWERS process. She was highly committed to living her best life, after having spent years with significant outward success as an attorney, but having little internal satisfaction. She was on a roll, which ground to a screeching halt when we got to the point of identifying and actualizing her inner purpose. Karen was convinced that she didn't have an inner purpose. She had wrestled early on in her life with the idea of spirituality and the inner purpose. Ultimately, she had determined that she didn't have an inner purpose, even though it seemed to happen for other people. She could recognize alignment, flow and ease in others.

Despite her best efforts, she couldn't see it in herself. She also felt that she *should* have an inner purpose, and so she was monumentally stuck.

We started with the two Jack Canfield questions. Answering them was slow going. Karen had a hard time trying to identify the qualities that uniquely represented her. She saw her success and abilities as generic—no different than any other person's. When she tried to make a list of experiences that brought her joy, she stalled—out of gas, flat tires, stuck on the side of the road.

Karen was encountering one of the most common blocks that can occur at this point in the EMPOWERS process, and she started to feel worse. The more she tried to come up with an activity or an experience that she felt passionate about and that lit her inner spark, the less energy she had to move forward. She said it felt like when the battery died in her car—she kept turning the key and pumping the gas, but nothing happened. Worse yet, she was ready to give up and walk away. She said, "Maybe it's me. Maybe I just don't have a passion or a purpose, other than my job. Maybe I've just been kidding myself all along."

Luckily, we were able to move her past that point, thanks to a summer rainstorm. Karen had been driving to meet with me. It was a very hot, humid day and she had forgotten to take off her suit jacket before she got in the car. She was sweltering, and the air conditioning wasn't making enough of a difference. She had been on the phone with a colleague from work about an unexpected snafu, and her frustration was mounting by the minute. Plus, she had forgotten her bottle of ice water on her desk in her rush to leave the office. None of that was tragic, but in conjunction with her recent struggle to find her passion, she was hot, tired, disheartened, and cranky. The final straw was not finding parking close to the building. She had to park in the overflow lot and, as she exited her car, the heavens opened and it began to rain. It was one of those times when the sun is shining at the same time the rain is pouring down. Karen started to make a run for the building... and then it happened. She realized that the summer rain was cooling her heated skin. She breathed a huge sigh of relief, as her tension started to melt away. As she continued her walk toward the building, she noticed a small child across the street splashing barefoot in the newly formed puddles and laughing with abandon. Karen stopped then and stood in the rain, soaking up the uncomplicated enjoyment, the unfettered joy, of that child. She remembered similar moments in her own life—moments when she had been totally, happily, caught up in the freedom of play. As those memories surfaced, Karen began to really notice how she felt in that moment. She felt the sun on her face and the cooling rain at the same time. She noticed her smile and her a strong urge to take off her shoes and splash through puddles.

Karen came in a few minutes late to our appointment, dripping wet and with an enormous smile on her face. As she told me the story, her face lit up and she started to laugh. "I've been making it so hard. I thought there was some kind of special, impossible-to-imagine feeling that would tell me, *This is joy. This is passion. This is your purpose*, but just now, out in the parking lot, *I got it*. It's about *my* perceptions—what creates a feeling of freedom and lightness inside me, not what someone else thinks is a passion. And my passion, or one of them, is being in nature. I *love* being outside. That is how I can make my soul sing."

Try This

Sit or lie in a comfortable position. Begin using the breathing techniques we've discussed. Really pay attention as your breath comes in and goes out. Allow yourself to settle down, and whenever your attention wonders, bring it back to the sensation of your breath coming in and going out. (You are doing meditation. Yay!) Bring the idea of love to mind. Think of circumstances, situations, people, places, or things you feel or have felt love for. Keep breathing, and let the experience of love fill you up. Now think of the things you have done with love. Think of what you've done that has brought you joy. Think of whatever causes you to smile on the inside. Let your mind consider what you love, what makes you smile, what brings you joy, and imagine doing more of whatever that is. Remind yourself that doing more of what brings you joy is like bringing in sunshine and watering the inner seedling of your purpose. Let it flourish and grow. *This* is your inner purpose.

Let's go back to Sandi. Why was she having such a hard time identifying her inner purpose? If it's so easy to do, why wasn't that intelligent, successful, committed-to-self-growth woman able to figure it out? Sandi could and did figure it out, but she got waylaid along the way. She had spent so many years nurturing the growth of doubt, fear, not feeling ready, and not feeling good enough that she had been feeding the weeds and not the seedlings. Sandi was afraid of being wrong and was stuck looking and waiting for external validation of her inner purpose. She had lost sight of her own value and only saw her inner light as reflected through others. She was trying to follow someone else's path—or, rather, her *perception* of someone else's path—and had turned away from the beacon of her own inner light of purpose. She felt like she was adrift on a stormy sea with no way to get to shore, no realizing that she had been safely anchored all the time—just by being herself.

As we began to address Sandi's search for inner purpose, she had a powerful realization. She has always been a firm believer in the idea that "everything happens for a reason," but she wasn't applying it to her own situation. Sandi had been looking at the events of her life as if they were the negative outcomes of her not finding her way or not being good enough. Each time that she took two steps backward, she took it as further proof that there was something lacking in her. That belief had become so entrenched that she couldn't envision a different perspective.

What was the big reveal for Sandi? Like a lightning bolt (but really as a result of doing all the rest of her work), she realized that she had needed distance (which took the form of challenging life experiences and disappointments) in order to see the forest for the trees. Sandi had been so caught up in the details of everything that happened (wandering among trees in a dense forest) that whenever she came upon a little clearing or a patch of sunny sky (her internal connections with her inner purpose), she appreciated it, but attributed its real value as the *external reaction* she got from others about it.

Here's an example. Sandi has always loved to cook. She loves to experiment with different recipes, and feeding her family and friends is an act of love—an expression of her inner purpose. But Sandi didn't see that because she didn't see the value of her cooking *for herself.* She knew cooking was something she loved to do and that brought her joy. She enjoyed the compliments when a meal was well received, and felt disheartened when her children preferred macaroni and cheese. *Sandi believed that engaging with her inner purpose would be evident and noticed by other people.* She didn't realize that the only validation, the only opinion or notice that mattered, was her own. When she realized that living her inner purpose was about doing what fed her soul and brought her joy, her light exploded into brilliance. She didn't change a lot of the things she was already doing, but boy did her soul shine brightly.

Connecting to and engaging with her inner purpose altered Sandi's entire perspective of the world. She stepped into living a life of ease—allowing herself to see and value *who she was,* looking inside herself for validation. When new challenges or struggles arose, she made sure she had a rescue plan in place to remind her of her ability to see the forest, not only the trees. In our last session, Sandi shared her newest favorite Rumi quote: "When you do things from your soul, you feel a river moving in you, a joy."

↦↦- ❬❬❬

This chapter focused on going within, and then letting out, the things that bring you *joy.* If you've been reading through without doing the exercises, or if you've had the sneaky suspicion that joy isn't accessible for you, don't worry. You absolutely do have the capacity for joy, which is the essential key to discovering your inner purpose. Sometimes our dreams and passions get buried under the avalanche of life circumstances, but that doesn't mean they're not there. *Patience*, which is a form of self-compassion and one of your core happiness ingredients, and *staying present* (as you learned about in Chapter 5) will move that piled-up avalanche of debris faster than you may expect. If you're feeling resistance, you're definitely ready for the next chapter, where you'll Release the Blocks and Go for It.

Chapter 10
R—Release the Blocks and Go for It.

"Don't let the fear of striking out hold you back."
Babe Ruth

Wouldn't it be great if we could simply decide to move forward with a plan and disregard the fear and doubt that pops up before we've taken a single step? Doesn't it sound wonderful? Wouldn't it be wonderful to step up to bat without worrying about whether we will be good enough; to swing at each pitch with our whole hearts, instead of saying, "I'll sit this one out"; to not have the stress of taking a risk; to be so confident that there's no thought of failure? I have wished for that many times, and I'm sure you have, too.

Even though I know that a little uncertainty brings about the good kind of stress and keeps me motivated and moving toward my goals and my dreams, it's too easy for the good stress to morph into bad stress and undermine the process. It's sort of like cholesterol: You want the good cholesterol to be higher and the bad cholesterol to be lower. To take that a step further, there's a problem when either the good cholesterol is too low, or the bad cholesterol is too high. If *both* are out of balance—*wham*. There's definitely a need for some kind of intervention.

Fear is the number one block to your success, and that little bugger is *sneaky*. Just when you think you're all set, that you've climbed the mountain of fear and gotten to the top, fear pops up and says, "Don't fall" or "How are you going to get back down?" or "So you climbed a mountain. Big deal. There are ten more ahead." Worst of all is when fear whispers to you that you've wasted your time, or that no one cares, or that you're *still* not good enough. Struggling with fear is common. The object of fear may shift over time, but I don't know of anyone who has completely obliterated all fear from their life (the tiniest little bit of fear is okay, as long as it isn't growing too fast and taking over).

In the beginning of this book, I offered a peek into the purpose of this chapter, and I want to repeat here a bit of what I said then: "This step is about recognizing that fear has a hiding place inside you, and acknowledging that with compassion and conviction. It doesn't work to run away from fear, because then you can be attacked from behind. It doesn't work to put up your fists and fight fear, because it's too slippery and it shape-shifts. The key to vanquishing the debilitating effects of fear is to embrace it, claim it, and invite it in for dinner (but not for an extended stay)." What does it mean to acknowledge fear with compassion and conviction? It means taking the advice of Eleanor Roosevelt and doing "one thing each day that scares you," without beating yourself up for having the fear in the first place. It means taking a breath, giving yourself a mental (or actual) hug, and saying to yourself, *Of course I'm scared. That's okay. Let's do this anyway.* It means recognizing when the fear is like an enormous woodpile, and moving the pieces of wood one at a time. Overcoming fear is usually not an immediate process. I mean, if you could snap your fingers and banish fear, then wouldn't you have done it before now?

Dealing with fear involves recognizing that fear plays an important role in your life. Fear can wake you up and cause you to notice and pay attention to the potential threat. Too much fear can cause you to freeze in your tracks or run away (those automatic stress responses again). When you notice fear, acknowledge its presence, and keep breathing even when it requires a whole bunch of self-talk, you are on the road to developing a working co-existence with fear. When you take the opportunity to know and understand what you fear, you start to decrease the power fear holds over you. *You can tell yourself, Yeah, fear, I know you're there. That's okay. I also know you're not actually going to kill me.*—even if it *feels* like you are in a life-threatening situation. We're not talking here about actual danger. This is about the fear of the unknown, the fear of failing, the fear of not measuring up, the fear of truly being awesome, and the fear of the changes that will bring about in your life. If you move into a more collaborative working relationship with fear, things in your life *will* change—fast. Without the tethering effect of fear, you will be able to take action in all sorts of areas, including some you weren't even aware of.

Linda had an interesting relationship with fear. She'd learned early in her childhood that if she showed fear to others, that usually brought about a negative outcome. She'd also learned that standing up to fears brought about by external circumstances worked really well for her. Everyone who knew her described her as fearless because of these two lessons she'd learned. But internally it was a whole different story. Internally, Linda believed that she had to make everyone else happy and meet everyone else's needs—usually at the expense of her own—or she would be left all alone. The biggest thing that frightened Linda was being alone. Nevertheless, for many years, Linda led what appeared to be a fabulous life. She had a great job working as an attorney at a major firm, a husband and children she adored, fantastic friends and extended family. Everything was wonderful... until it wasn't.

Linda's fear of being alone led her to work too much, give too much, and put up with too much. And she just kept paying the price, because the cost of the alternative—being alone—seemed way too high. She was afraid. Over time, that fear grew and grew and grew. It grew so big that when things started to really go downhill in her marriage, she stayed. And when it got worse, she buckled down and tried harder. Because anything, even a really bad situation, was better than being alone. Fear had taken over, and she couldn't see any options other than doing more of the same, and doing it faster and for longer. Linda knew that wasn't working and that she was stuck.

When we began to work together, Linda started by identifying little actions she could take to recognizing and accept the fear. One stick of wood at a time, she began to move that pile of fear. She took the action of inviting fear in for dinner and started to get to really know it. That wasn't always easy (fear is a demanding guest), but she had realized that fear was a *guest*, and that it was up to her to figure out how long fear was welcome to stay.

Along the way, Linda realized that there were lots of times that she *preferred* to be alone. Solitude helped her to recover from too many social interactions. She loved to be out in nature by herself. She felt very spiritually connected when she took a walk in the woods or at the beach. It struck her that she loved the long drives by herself that she had to take for work. With all of that, the face of her fear changed.

Linda recognized that if she stopped being afraid of being alone—which she discovered that she actually liked—then she would want a lot of other things in her life to change. She saw the ways that treating her fear with compassion, instead of yelling at herself for feeling that way, allowed her to imagine what was possible beyond the fear. She used that realization to alter significant aspects of her life. She changed her job. She stopped jumping to fulfill everyone else's requests. She left her marriage. She took a job in which she was highly compensated and appreciated for her amazing professional skills and talents. She spent time with people who added to her life, and she spent a lot less time with people who were a drain on her energy. She spent time alone, and she also entered into a positive relationship. She still had doubts and moments of insecurity and fear, but she had learned to keep the fear as a part of her, rather than letting it control the whole of her. How did Linda change her relationship with fear? She didn't simply say, "Okay, I see you. Come on in." She'd been aware of fear all along, so the presence of it wasn't a huge revelation. As we worked together, though, she saw more of the ways fear had gotten in the way, since it had hidden under all sorts of masks. She learned to identify fear crouched down behind *I can't, It won't work, I'm too tired,* and *I don't know how.* She saw the shadow of fear underneath those and exposed it to light. She became a master at sniffing out all the false faces of fear (what we often think of as excuses).

But Linda also used a specific technique to uncover fear. She used the powerful magic of manifestation, also known as quantum physics. In Dr. Joe Dispenza's book, *Breaking the Habit of Being Yourself,* and on his website, he makes complicated science and philosophy understandable. He writes about changing from the inside out, moving from thought patterns and a *perception* of reality to living a different *actual* reality. Dr. Dispenza completely caught my interest with this passage (emphasis mine): "The latest research supports the notion that we have a natural ability to change the brain and body by thought alone, so that it looks biologically like some future event has already happened. Because *you can make thought more real than anything else*, you can change who you are from brain cell to gene, given the right understanding."

What Dr. Dispenza is referring to is the scientific understanding that thoughts are not separate from matter. He is describing the amazing power that your mind has on the external world. For a comprehensive explanation of how this works (addressing energy fields, atoms, electrons, and particles), you can read his books. For the EMPOWERS process, what you need to know is that *when you envision something, you are creating the reality of it.* Since we aren't used to thinking in that way, we get stuck in our ordinary patterns of thinking. We think we know what's real and how things work, but that limits us in what we perceive. Our perceptions then limit what we do to the same set of actions and reactions we have already learned. When you create a different version of what you would like to happen; when you really believe it's not only possible, that's true. But when you make what you would like to happen a multi-sensory experience—bringing your visualization alive by seeing, smelling, tasting, hearing, and feeling the desired outcome in your imagination—you are actually creating a new template for electrons to follow. Or, as Dr. Dispenza says, "…if you can imagine a future event in your life based on any one of your personal desires, that reality already exists as a possibility in the quantum field, waiting to be observed by you." When you observe a possibility, you are bringing it into existence.

Linda used this process to create the life she wanted, without fear running the show. She didn't just sit down and say to herself, *Okay, I want it to be better* or *No more fear*, although those are good early baby steps. She constructed a detailed, explicit vision of what she wanted her life to be like, incorporating as many sensory aspects as possible. Then she spent time putting herself *into that reality.* She would sit quietly and build that internal visualization as vibrantly as she could. She kept doing that, and she began to notice the little building blocks falling into place. Pretty soon, she was seeing enormous differences in her life. Naturally, fear showed up to try and derail the process, but since she had already made her peace with fear (mostly), she stayed on track. And it worked.

I have used this process myself, with amazing results. For example, I was working at a job that involved a long commute, which was sucking the life out of me one hour at a time. I tried everything—listening to inspiring audio books, talking to friends during my commute, seeing the drive as my "quiet time"—and while I made those things helped to make it more tolerable, the commute was still a daily drain. In many ways, the commute was really a surface excuse. The bigger issue, my underlying fear, was that I didn't feel fulfilled, and I needed to make a change. I was scared. With that job I had security and familiarity, and it "wasn't that bad." I loved most of the work I did. So I spent a couple of years "making the best of it," instead of dealing with my fear. I was trying to barricade the door against fear, but I was the one trapped inside. One day (while driving, of course), I said out loud, "Okay universe I'm ready. Bring it on." I immediately broke into a cold sweat and was terrified of what I had just done. If this manifesting stuff was true, what had I set in motion? I hadn't triggered anything cataclysmic, since I hadn't yet figured out what I wanted instead, but the door had been opened.

After the first tide of fear swept in, I began to consider what I wanted. Instead of saying *I want X job at Y place*, I developed a set of criteria of what I wanted. They included a short commute (obviously), maintaining my same lifestyle, doing work that motivated and inspired me, helping others to realize their best selves and live better lives, and teaching. Cut to six months later when I was offered a job fifteen minutes from my home, doing work that inspired others and that challenged and interested me, helping others develop their skills and talents. It included teaching. And a *lot* more free time—no commute—to expand the work I wanted to do in the areas of personal development, coaching, supervision, and writing. Bingo.

That new job happened through the creative use of "what if." Instead of the common use of "what if"—the one where you say, *What if I don't get the job? What if I can't pay my rent? What if no one at the party talks to me?*—that is centered around a negative assumption, I used a positive-oriented version. My "what if" was something like, *What if I could do whatever I wanted? What if I had lots of free time to do what I love? What if I wasn't afraid?* This is an extremely powerful process, and it's the first step in creating a new reality. Once you can face your fear, call it out, and *imagine* not being afraid, miracles start to happen. Add some somatic visualization (see it, hear it, feel it, taste it) into the mix, and you have created your personalized recipe for manifestation. It's seems absolutely crazy, but it works.

I will share a secret with you about how I know *for sure* when fear is creeping up behind me and it's time to turn around and face it with courage and compassion. Ready? I feel like I'm going to vomit. Big-time. My chest gets tingly, with a swirling sort of sensation, and my throat tightens up. I feel a wave of nausea from thinking about a scary risk or opportunity. It sets off a chain reaction of thoughts, mostly centered around why I *shouldn't* do whatever I was contemplating doing. It's not comfortable, but it's an awesome sign, and I can't ignore it.

If I step further along the road of pushing that risk or opportunity away, through *Not now* or *This won't work*, then the feeling subsides. But if I move right to the end of the high diving board and get ready to jump—the nauseous feeling is back, full force. That is the moment when I feel the most trapped and can become frozen.

Imagine a super high diving board that extends out over a lake. You've waited in line, and now it's your turn. As you walk to the end of the board, the fear feeling starts to emerge. You don't want to do this. It was a stupid idea. You are ready to turn around and climb down off this ridiculously high diving board and go sit quietly and safely on the beach. There's only one problem. There's a huge group of people waiting to jump in line behind you. They are all in different places on the ladder, blocking your easy escape route. One of them is even right there on the board behind you. Going back is not an option. Going forward is terrifying. You start to feel like you're going to puke. Or collapse. There's no magical rescue. It's up to you. You've got to jump. It's scary, but it's the only way forward. You take a couple of breaths (excellent delaying tactic, but also calming). You remind yourself that it's okay, that you're not going to die. You recognize the fearful feelings flooding your body, you acknowledge them... and you jump.

Warning—the feeling of jumping, taking a risk, will likely still be there as you stagger out of the water onto the beach. It's the residual effect of the stress hormones that raced through your body. But there's also another feeling. You're relieved (*I did it!*), and there's a tiny bit of pride. The more you think about the *accomplishment,* rather than the *anticipation,* the better you feel. You're alive and you freaking did it! You are a rock star. It doesn't matter that an obnoxious kid four years younger than you keeps racing up, diving off, and doing it again. That's his deal, not yours. You did the thing that scared you, and you survived.

When I feel that nauseous feeling start bubbling up inside, I know I'm on the right track. My body is being my friend, showing me that this action is important to me—that it matters, for whatever reason. It's giving me an opportunity to stay in the moment and *live my life.* And you know what? It has never steered me wrong. *Every single time* I felt it, I was on the verge of a life-changing action, even when I didn't know it at the time. It's my secret sign to go for it, and to embrace my rock star self.

I've given you the steps, with supporting examples, of how you can live a life of purpose, passion, and ease. I've shown you how to tell *stress* goodbye, and welcome in *happy* with open arms. There's no special club or secret handshake necessary. It's all here in the book. The question is: Will you do it? Or will you tell yourself it may work for someone else, but not for you? Will you hunker down in a bunker of fear and keep on keeping on as you are? Will you create a long list of all the reasons why you will, just not right now? Will you tell yourself this is a bunch of crap and you're too busy, too stressed, too tired to take action? Or will you be sidelined by thinking that maybe you don't have enough "proof" yet that this process works?

In my experience of working with myself and others, you will do at least one—and likely most—of those avoidance behaviors at some point in the EMPOWERS process. It's inevitable. That doesn't mean you can't implement this process—not at all. It means that you are human, and that we make mistakes. We start to try something and we falter. We encounter a bump and see it as a failure and stop the whole thing. You will do this, too.

I have employed every single one of those progress-busting techniques, as well as many alternate versions. Every person I have worked with either started out with those negative beliefs, encountered them when change was imminent, or both (usually both). Most of us are resistant to change, even when we have had enough and want to change. A body at rest tends to stay at rest. And we are masters at creating reasons why change can't and won't happen. Despite that, change is not only possible it's totally achievable—as you can see from the stories of Theresa, Bethany, Sandi, Karen, and Linda. Even when you're afraid, change is possible. In the words of Harriet Tubman, "Every great dream begins with a dreamer. Always remember, you have within you the strength, the patience, and the passion to reach for the stars to change the world." Now seems like a good time to start.

Try This

Find a quiet place to sit or lie down (you know the drill). Take a few deep breaths. Begin to breathe normally and focus on your inhales and exhales. After several rounds of breathing, ask yourself the questions, *What if I could do, be, or have anything?* and *What would I do if I were not afraid?* Let yourself sit with these questions. If you don't have immediate answers, that's totally fine. This is an exercise to practice several times, until you begin to get a glimmer of what you want your future to look like.

Chances are, you already know some answers to those questions, but you've decided that they're not possible to pursue. Suspend your disbelief to give yourself the chance to hear your answers from within.

Once you've got a mental picture of what you want, make it a multi-sensory, vibrant delight of a visualization. Add as much sensory detail as possible. Feel the atmosphere, the temperature of a scene of your best life. Add in color, smell, and taste. What do you hear? What do you see? What does it feel like to make it Technicolor, HD, real? Cement this vision in your mind, and then return to it over and over. Add in more details, more flourishes, more joy. Believe in it. Taste it. Make it real.

⤜⤛⤚⤙

I've shared some really inspiring stories about women who have made major shifts in how they think, feel, and perceive. Those women flipped the script but kept the parts that most mattered regarding their own skills, desires, and values. Each of those women encountered significant blocks along the way.

This chapter has reviewed the most common places people get stuck and ways to forge a path through the weeds. This is such an important chapter, because you will be there at some point, too: envisioning what you want and facing your fears. Encountering challenges and obstacles is one of the ways we know we're still alive.

Utilizing the knowledge and skills you've developed through the EMPOWERS process is how you move through whatever comes your way. And that leads to the final step, where you get to Shine Your Light Brightly.

Chapter 11
S—Shine Your Light Brightly

To shine your brightest light is to be who you truly are.
Roy T. Bennett

O h, yes, you *are* a rock star. You've done *so* much work. You have increased your energy, made more time for yourself (yay, self-care!), and made time for the passions and purposes that are bubbling out of you. You know what it's like to be your own best friend, and you are putting that into practice every day. Manifestation and perspective are on the way to becoming second nature. You are an empowered rock star, and you are moving forward with confidence and ease.

This part of the EMPOWERS process is all about celebration and ways to keep the party going. It's about the songs, the words, the images that will sustain you and excite you and inspire.

Hang on. Are you are still asking yourself if you can do this, make big steps toward a better life? Have you made some steps forward but feel there's more to be done? You are not alone. Even though Chapter 10 was about the resistance and blocks that can and do show up, the topic of celebrating yourself is another place that may be a stumbling block.

Have you ever put something in the oven for the specified amount of time and then found it wasn't quite done? I did that the other day with a quiche. I followed the directions, set the timer, and was ready and waiting (and salivating) for my delicious meal. It was such a disappointment when I took the first bite and discovered the middle was runny and the bottom crust was soggy. Apparently, it needed a little more heat to be completely cooked. From the outside, it looked perfect. There was no way to tell it wasn't finished until I started to dig in.

That was exactly what Vicky encountered. She had gone through all the other steps of the EMPOWERS process, but when it came to shining her light, she faltered. She had been on a high, implementing changes right and left, seeing manifestations all through her life. She was feeling energized, enlightened, and self-loving. She had identified her signature strengths and was incorporating new methods of using them at work and at home. On the surface, everything looked great. Her life was out of the oven and ready to be served, with excitement and well-deserved pride. And then the call came in. She was offered the opportunity to do something *big*, something she had only recently started to visualize. And she hesitated.

During our session, Vicky told me a story about her husband painting their bathroom the previous year. "We went with a really bold color. We got all new fixtures, new towels, the whole shebang. It looked wonderful. Until I got into the tub and noticed that he hadn't finished the trim around the cabinets. You couldn't see it unless you were in the bathtub. I complimented him on doing a fantastic job, and then I asked him to finish the last little piece. Do you know it's been almost a year, and it's still not done? I've never understood why he would stop right before the last finishing touch. But that's how I feel now. Everything's going well, things are looking good and getting better, but I don't feel able to do the last little piece of work to pull it all together."

Vicky was in that familiar place of needing to seal the deal but having second thoughts about her ability to handle what came next. Instead of relying on what she had learned so far, she started to back off, opening the floodgates to all sorts of questions. *What if this is all a fluke? What if I can't do this? What if I don't have any more inspiration after I take the last step? What if this isn't* really *what I'm supposed to do?* Her thoughts chased themselves around and around, and negativity was starting to leak into every area of her life. In our session, she unloaded all those thoughts and more. She had started to wonder if she had bitten off more than she could chew, and she was terrified she was going to "choke and die."

Interestingly, just before Vicki and I were scheduled to meet, I read a story about a woman who had written and self-published an amazing, much-needed book. She had put *tons* of heart and soul into birthing her book-baby, but then she never did any marketing or promotion. At all. Even though her former and current clients loved the content of the book and had benefitted from her knowledge and expertise. Even though there was a huge market for her book, and it would likely help thousands of women. That woman let her book sit for *two years* because, in her words, "I'm part lazy and part afraid of who knows what." I understood that woman. She *wasn't* lazy—not at all. She wouldn't have gotten her book done if she had been lazy. She wasn't bored, washed-up, lacking, or not good enough. But she did get part of it right: She was afraid. That's what kept her from taking the last step. I don't personally know that woman, and I've taken some liberties above about her inner life, but I'm confident that her fears were causing the block, not any actual laziness. I say that because I have seen it happen *so many times.*

I shared that woman's story with Vicky, and it really resonated with her. "Yes. That's me *exactly*, and that's even better than my bathroom tale. But what did that woman do next? What do *I* do? I don't want all of this work I've done to be for nothing." Vicky could recognize her fear, but she struggled making sense of it. She knew it was time to jump off the diving board, and she'd thought she was prepared. She had conquered the fears that came up while climbing the ladder, as well as the fears that showed up once she stepped onto the diving board platform. She had addressed her concerns about jumping into cold water, and she had learned how to swim. She'd thought she was *ready*. Her foot was raised, poised to go. "It just doesn't make sense," she said "Why *now*? Shouldn't I have dealt with this already?"

Vicky had unpeeled another layer of the onion, of the process of change. After following all the directions and cooking herself anew for the "right" amount of time, she wanted to be done. It rocked her world when she discovered there was more. But, guess what? There's *always* more.

This book and the EMPOWERS process aren't meant to be your final steps. If you're alive, there's more. The EMPOWERS process is what gets you moving down the road following your purpose and your passion, *and that will evolve*. This process is a way to carve out the crap that gets in the way, so you can focus on what you need to *know* and *do* to be your best self. This is a process to bring ease to what you've already mastered, so you can embrace your vision. It's unbelievably rewarding, fulfilling, awesome—and scary beyond belief. The fear that comes with taking risks on yourself and for yourself is terrifying. That's a *good* thing, because it matters that you do it. Who you are, what you think, the choices you make *must* matter to you for you to keep going forward. But the more you peel the onion, the stronger the smell, the more you are tempted to back off and stop peeling. Even at the very last minute, when you are poised for big success. If you're me, that's when you absolutely, *totally* want to vomit.

The *I don't know why* of the fear that surfaces is all about success. Both the blow-your-socks-off kind of success ("What do I know about how to live as a total rock star?") and the crash-and-burn kind of success, sometimes referred to as "failure" ("I tanked. I screwed this up. I didn't get the promotion/job/date/praise. How can I go on?"). Except all those situations *are* about success, because you learn by what goes well and you learn (usually more) by what doesn't go well. The only thing you learn when you stop just short of the finish line is what it feels like to stop from fear. The craziest thing about it is—*you already know that*. You have stopped because of fear before, and those are the things you list as regrets. *Those* are the moments that keep you awake, wondering why you're missing out.

Whenever I hit those moments (after I get my nausea under control), I listen to "Try Everything," Shakira's song from the movie *Zootopia* (check out the full lyrics; they're completely inspiring). If you want to truly live a life of purpose, passion and ease, welcome in the *full* experience; welcome in the fear and nausea, *as well as* the joy and excitement.

My all-time favorite personal coach, Angela Lauria, recently shared her version of this: "I celebrate the victories. I am as proud of my failures as I am of my successes. I choose my failures and I choose my wins. *Relentlessly. This is the work that leads to success.*" Oh, yeah. That's a woman who is shining her light *super bright*. She doesn't stop and turn around at the end of the diving board. She jumps—and learns from what happens next. If her quiche is runny in the middle, then she knows to cook it longer the next time. And she markets the hell out of her expertise. She is *owning* her light, amping up the brightness, and replacing the bulb with a stronger wattage whenever necessary.

I shared Angela's story and words with Vicky, and she *got it*. She took a few deep breaths, then a few more. She swallowed and shook her head back and forth. Finally, she said, "Okay, I'm ready. I might puke, but I'm ready."

What happens after you make the promise to yourself to keep going and to share your shining light? Let's look at a few options.

Commit

First, you make *and keep* the commitment to yourself to *truly live your best life.* You are worth your own best efforts, and if you don't make that commitment, no one else can make it for you. *You* are responsible for your own thoughts, feelings, and actions (and you are not responsible for the thoughts, feelings, and actions of anyone else.) This EMPOWERS process isn't a quick-fix commitment, like a three-day juice cleanse. This is a commitment to integrating the concepts and techniques from the last seven chapters on a long-term (think permanent) basis. If this sounds like a big step to you, *don't panic.* The commitment is internal, and it doesn't cost anything except the shedding of old patterns and habits. These process steps are the building blocks of the life you want, a life designed to your specifications. They form a solid foundation, and there's still lots of room for creativity.

Try This

Make a playlist of at least twelve songs that reflect your new attitude. I created a song list for you before I started writing this book (you can find the access link at the end of the book). I turned on this playlist *every single time* I sat down to write, because I wanted all the manifesting mojo possible to be behind these words. I was envisioning *your* success before we even met. These are all songs that celebrate you and your progress. The songs I chose for you reflect your thriving, your individuality, your knowledge of who you really are, your hidden superpowers, and your ability to defy gravity (song hint there).

Pay Attention

Second, pay attention to the words of Katy Perry: "I don't negotiate with insecurities." Those creepy, annoying, *It can't be true for me* thoughts are out the door. There's no room at the inn, and there's no light left on to welcome them in. They've gotta go. The thoughts of *I can't*, *It won't work*, *It's not for me*, and those negative *What ifs* are only different versions of *I'm afraid*. You've already decided you want more. You've already made a commitment to yourself to keep your flame alive and glowing. This step in the EMPOWERS process is about helping you do that by keeping your spirits up.

Here are a few key actions to help you reinforce your commitment and your motivation, and to pay attention to the process in a way that supports you:

- Every day, identify at least three good things that you are grateful for, *in that day.*
- Take time to breathe, really *breathe*, at least three times a day.
- Ask yourself, *What can I learn from this situation?*
- At least once a day, consider your perspective by asking yourself, *What does this situation look like through the eyes of my best self?*

Using language and words to support the process is also a great way to expand and broaden your perspective. To help you out, I've pulled together an A-Z list of words that reflect concepts, values, ideas, and changes that support your ongoing progress (you can find the access link at the end of the book).

An easy way to use the list is to pick two to three words per week from it and work them into your routine. They are words that you can use in conversation, as well as words you can implement through your behavior. I recommend picking words from different parts of the alphabet.

For example, you might pick Affirm, Invigorate, and Unconditional for one week. So, as you're walking to your car when it's below freezing, you can remind yourself that a brisk walk is *invigorating* and gets your blood pumping. Not only is this a way of practicing the perspective you want in the moment, but *affirming* your desire to be conscious of moments of gratitude is a *lot* better than being miserable, cranky, and tired. And it makes the walk go faster). *Unconditional* can be a part of almost every day. For example, you can accept your efforts on a recent project with *unconditional* love and compassion, rather than aiming for perfection, which isn't possible. Or you can set aside time to allow yourself to engage in your passion *unconditionally*, recognizing that living your passion and purpose enhances the life of everyone around you.

If you feel that this is a little like having a vocabulary assignment from when you were little and told to "use the word in a sentence," then, yeah, it pretty much is. The purpose of those assignments was to help you learn the meanings of new words and to incorporate them into your everyday language. Today, you know the meanings of lots of words, but you may not have been *applying* them in your life—especially a lot of the positive and encouraging ones. It's time to do that.

Shine

Third—get out there and *find ways to shine your light*. Have you ever seen a vigil or a service where people were lighting candles? It's usually dark when it starts. One person lights a candle, and you see that tiny little glimmer of light. The first person lights a second candle, the second person lights a third. Moment by moment, the room becomes brighter as more candles shine, pushing back the darkness. From a single pinpoint, light expands and grows, candle by candle. You can see the connections being made and passed. It's a beautiful, moving process.

When all the candles have been lit, the amount of light is amazing. You know, deep in your soul, that *you are not alone*. And each person's light reflects all the others, giving a super-powered boost across the board. That's what you do when you follow the EMPOWERS process and unveil your phenomenal light to the world. By being the courageous-in-fear *real* you—the authentic, perfectly imperfect, in-the-flesh you who honors personal responsibility by moving forward—you add brilliance to the universe. Letting your inner spark be seen, shares the flame with everyone around you. As your light grows, their light grows, and light it spreads and expands.

The universe needs you and your light. So, take the risks to bring your light into the open. Don't only practice shining in your bedroom, or keep your fabulous ideas confined to your journal. What are the next steps you need to take to shine more? How are you going to put your passion into action? How are you going to live your inner purpose in the world? What seems like it's out of reach or "too much" to try? Instead of creating a list of reasons for failure, start *making it happen*. Keep in mind that you will struggle and you will fall, but each time you get up and start again, you're adding to the brilliance of your light. Each time you rise, with full commitment and accountability, you add to the light of the world.

Try This

This is super fun. Create a visual representation of what you love and want in your life—the things that bring you joy, or that have seemed out of reach, or that represent the transformed you. I did one of these to represent how you may have felt before starting the EMPOWERS process—basically, the feelings and thoughts that prompted you to pick up this book and read it. But I also created a montage of how I see you *after* this process. Boy, do you look fabulous. You are amazing, wonderful, strong, clear, and inspiring. You've always been this way, but you didn't see it as clearly. *Rock star* is just the beginning—you are on *fire.*

Shining your light brightly is the culmination of your work in the EMPOWERS process. This is the step that illuminates all your progress and allows you to see clearly where you've been and where you're headed. This marks the beginning of your brand-new, fulfilled, happy, resilient and productive life. You've faced the unknown and the seemingly impossible with courage (and maybe some nausea) and continued forward anyway. You've learned to embrace "failure" for the opportunities to grow, and you've reveled in the satisfaction of knowing you are fully responsible for your choices.

You are ready for the final chapter, ready to be On Your Way.

Chapter 12
On Your Way

When you started this journey, I promised you a few things. You wanted to stop feeling tired, stressed, overwhelmed, and as if you were missing out. You knew you wanted to increase your happiness, resilience, and productivity. I promised to show you simple solutions to help you move into living with ease, being your best self, living with purpose and passion, and turning on your inner rock star. In each chapter, you've learned specific techniques to address all of those issues, as well as exercises to put the theories into action.

You have integrated new knowledge or refreshed your knowledge about the mechanisms of stress and how to make this process, the process of positive and empowering change, work *for* you instead of against you, by utilizing breathing, mindfulness, perspective shifts, and gratitude (even though you thought you were anti-meditation). You've redefined *success* and *failure* in the context of choices and boundaries. You identified your signature strengths and explored how to leverage them to connect with your inner purpose and passion. You've re-invigorated old dreams and discovered brand new ones. You've made a new best friend (yourself!) and you're keeping her around and treating her with kindness, compassion, and love. You've let go of blocks and insecurities and are ready to light up the world with your inner glow.

You have done all of this, and that's fantastic. Now you have a roadmap to follow into your future. Like the best of today's GPS technologies, this roadmap comes with real-life updates. You will run into traffic jams, detours, construction delays, and interminable waits at railroad crossings. There is no getting around that. Sometimes a detour will take you to a temporary dead end. But by using the tools in the EMPOWERS process, you will navigate each obstacle with commitment. You have totally got this.

Keep in mind that *everyone* has days and times when the coffee is cold, someone cuts you off in traffic (triggering a stress reaction), and you've left your wallet at home. You may have days when you've got a headache, a cold, and a stomach ache all at once. And there will be losses, sorrow, and change. This is all part of the magic of being alive. If you've gotten off track, or if you've accidentally jumped back on the stress train and feel like you're going in the wrong direction, it's totally okay. Just go back to what you've learned, what you now know, and keep on truckin'.

These tools were made for using (to paraphrase Patsy Cline). Clear out your chakras, re-set your priorities, focus on what you need and what you love. Ask for and accept assistance, because when you are your own best friend, sometimes it takes a village to get things done. Celebrate everything from the minor (*I didn't spill my coffee*) to the major (*I've made my dream come true*). Stand tall in your magnificent, imperfect self, fully prepared with the knowledge that nothing stays the same and that there's always a new challenge, a new way to make your life more wonderful. Find a way to do *you*.

Maintain your commitment to living your best life and be proud of yourself. I am. *Your light illuminates my soul, and the world. Shine on.*

End Notes

Chapter 1

"Central command neurons of the sympathetic nervous system: basis of the fight-or-flight response," A. S. Jansen, X. Van Nguyen, V. Karpitskiy, T.C. Mettenleiter & A. D. Loewy, *Science*, 1995, vol. 270(5236), pg. 644.

"Exploring human freeze responses to a threat stressor," N. B. Schmidt, J.A. Richey, M. J. Zvolensky & J. K. Maner, *Journal of Behavior Therapy and Experimental Psychiatry*, 2008, vol. 39(3), pg. 292-304.

"Mechanisms linking early life stress to adult health outcomes," S. E. Taylor, *Proceedings of the National Academy of Sciences*, 2010, vol. 107(19), pg. 8507-8512.

"Positive psychology progress: empirical validation of interventions," M. E. Seligman, T. A. Steen, N. Park & C. Peterson, *American Psychologist*, 2005, vol. 60(5), pg. 410.

The Body Keeps the Score: Brain, Mind and Body in the Healing of Trauma, B. van der Kolk, Penguin Press, 2015, ISBN-10: 0143127748.

Why Zebras Don't Get Ulcers, Robert M. Sapolsky, Holt Paperbacks, 2004, ISBN-10: 0805073698.

Chapter 2

"Evaluation of the Mental Health Benefits of Yoga in a Secondary School: A Preliminary Randomized Clinical Trial," S. B. S. Khalsa, L. Hickey-Schultz, D. Cohen, N. Steiner & S. Cope, *Journal of Behavioral Health Services and Research,* 2012, vol. 39, pg. 80.

Flourish, M. E. P. Seligman, Atria Books, 2012, ISBN-10: 1439190763.

"The health benefits of yoga and exercise: a review of comparison studies," A. Ross & S. Thomas, *The Journal of Alternative and Complementary Medicine,* 2010, vol. 16(1), pg. 3-12.

Seligman, Martin, University of Pennsylvania, "Authentic Happiness"—www.authentichappiness.org. A plethora of positive psychology measurements to assess various aspects of happiness. The website is user friendly.

Chapter 3

Illusions: The Adventures of a Reluctant Messiah, R. Bach, Dell, 1989, ISBN 0440204887.

The Relaxation and Stress Reduction Handbook, M. Davis, E. Robbins Eshelman & M. McKay, New Harbinger Publications, 2008, ISBN-10: 1572245492.

Chapter 4

"Effects of a forgiveness intervention for older adults", M. Allemand, M. Steinerm & D. L. Hill, *Journal of Counseling Psychology*, Vol. 60(2), Pg. 279-286.

Awakening the Chakras: The Seven Energy Centers in Your Daily Life, V. Daniels, K. Daniels & P. Weltevrede, Inner Traditions/Bear, 2017, ISBN:1620555883.

"Exercise and well-being: a review of mental and physical health benefits associated with physical activity," F. Peneo & J. Dahn, *Current Opinion in Psychiatry*, 2005, vol. 18 (2), pg. 189-193.

How Stress Affects Your Health, American Psychological Association Fact Sheet, 2013, www.apa.org/helpcenter/stress.aspx.

"Positive psychology interventions: A meta-analysis of randomized controlled studies," B. Bolier, M. Haverman, G. Westerhof, H. Riper, F. Smit & E. Bohlmeijer, *BMC Public Health*, 2013.

Chapter 5

"Dynamic interplay of depression, perfectionism and self-regulation on procrastination," B. Uzun Ozer, J. O'Callaghan, A. Bokszczanin, E. Ederer & C. Essau, *British Journal of Guidance & Counselling*, 2014, vol. 42(3), pg. 309-319.

"Mindfulness-Based Stress Reduction and Health Benefits: A Meta-Analysis," P. Grossman, L. Niemann, S. Schmidt & H. Walach, *Journal of Psychosomatic Research*, 2004, vol. 57 (1), pg. 35-43.

"Multitasking Increases Stress and Insecure Behavior on Mobile Devices," Q. Liu, A.C. McLaughlin, B. Watson, W. Enck & A. Davis, *Proceedings of the Human Factors and Ergonomics Society Annual Meeting*, 2015, Vol. 59 (1), pg. 1110-1114.

"Task conflict effect in task switching," A. Braverman & N. Meiran, *Psychological Research*, 2010, vol. 74(6), pg. 568-578.

"The influence of perfectionism on procrastination in online graduate education students," G. Rakes & K. Dunn, *Proceedings of Society for Information Technology & Teacher Education International Conference*, 2014, pg. 799-803.

"Workplace based mindfulness practice and inflammation: a randomized trial," W. B. Malarkey, D. Jarjoura & M. Klatt, *Brain, Behavior, and Immunity*, 2013, vol. 27, pg. 145-154.

Fredrikson, Barbara—www.positivityratio.com Offers on-line tools including Positivity Self- Test and Social Connectedness Test with graph and score tracking of retake results over time; Loving Kindness and other guided meditations.

Chapter 6

"Counting Blessings versus Burdens: An Experimental Investigation of Gratitude and Subjective Well-Being in Daily Life," R. A. Emmons and M. E. McCullough, *Journal of Personality and Social Psychology*, 2013, Vol. 84, pg. 377-389.

"Counting Your Blessings: Positive memories among grateful persons," D.L. Grimm, Kolts, R. & P.C. Watkins, *Current Psychology: Developmental, Learning, Personality, Social*, 2004, vol. 23, pg. 52-67.

"Does mindfulness decrease stress and foster empathy among nursing students?," A. E. Beddoe & S. O. Murphy, *Journal of Nursing Education*, 2004, vol. 43(7), pg. 305-312.

"Effect of Pranyama on Physiological Variables," S. R. Mishra, A. Ghoshal & T. R. Patanaik, *International Journal of Scientific Research*, 2016, vol. 4 (10).

Positive Psychology in Practice: Promoting Human Flourishing in Work, Health, Education, and Everyday Life, S. Joseph (ed.), John Wiley & Sons, Inc., 2015

You Are a Badass: How to Stop Doubting Your Greatness and Start Living an Awesome Life, J. Sincero, Running Press, 2013, ISBN-10: 0762447699

Emmons Lab, UC Davis—www.psychologyucdavis.edu. Summaries of gratitude study findings. Gratitude Questionnaire, GQ-6.

Neff, Kristen—www.self-compassion.org. Self-compassion exercises, research studies, self-compassion questionnaire.

Chapter 7

"Positive affect and health," S. Cohen & S. Pressman, *Current Directions in Psychological Science*, 2006, vol. 15, pg. 122–125.

"Positive emotional style predicts resistance to illness after experimental exposure to rhinovirus or influenza a virus," S. Cohen, C. M. Alper, W. J. Doyle, J.J. Treanor & R. B. Turner, *Psychosomatic Medicine*, 2006, vol. 68(6), pg. 809-15.

"The confidence gap," K. Kay & C. Shipman, *The Atlantic*, 2014, vol. 14, pg. 1-18.

Miller, Richard—www.irest.us. Yogic deep relaxation downloads and research summaries.

Chapter 8

A Return to Love: Reflections on "A Course in Miracles," M. Williamson, Harper One, 1996, ISBN-10: 0060927488.

"Enhancing well-being and alleviating depressive symptoms with positive psychology interventions: A practice-friendly meta-analysis," N. L. Sin Sin & S. Lyubmirsky, *Journal of Clinical Psychology*, 2009, vol. 65(5), pg. 467-487.

The Four Agreements: A Practical Guide to Personal Freedom, Don Miguel Ruiz, Amber-Allen Publishing, 1997, ISBN-10: 1878424310.

Values in Action survey—www.viacharacter.org.

Chapter 9

EMDR for Clinician Self Care: Models, Scripted Protocols and Summary Sheets for Mental Heath Interventions, M. Luber (ed.), Springer Publishing Company, 2015, ISBN-10: 0826133398.

"The role of eye movement desensitization and reprocessing (EMDR) therapy in medicine: addressing the psychological and physical symptoms stemming from adverse life experiences," F. Shapiro, *The Permanente Journal*, 2014, vol. 18(1), pg. 71-77.

"The effectiveness of Emotional Freedom Techniques (EFT) for improving the physical, mental and emotional health of people with chronic diseases and/or mental health conditions: a systematic review protocol," M. Kalla & H. Khalil, *JBI Database of Systematic Reviews and Implementation Reports*, 2014, vol. 12(2), pg. 114-124.

"Reiki–Review of a Biofield Therapy History, Theory, Practice, and Research," P. Miles & T. Gala, *Alternative Therapies in Health and Medicine*, 2003, pg. 62-72.

The Success Principles: How to Get from Where You Are to Where You Want to Be, Jack Canfield, William Morrow Paperbacks, 10th Anniversary edition, 2015, ISBN-10: 0062364286.

Chapter 10

Breaking the Habit of Being Yourself: How to Lose Your Mind and Create a New One, Dr. Joe Dispenza, Hay House, 2013, ISBN-10: 1401938094.

"Doors Opening: A Mechanism for Growth After Adversity," A. M. Roepke & M. E. P. Seligman, *The Journal of Positive Psychology*, Vol. 10 (2), 2015.

Scioli, Anthony—www.gainhope.com. Information on various aspects of hope including related research findings; questionnaires for adults, teens & children.

Acknowledgments

"Happiness is a journey, not a destination"
Alfred D. Souza

This book has been a long time in coming. The idea of it has been a companion on my personal journey of discovery, self-love, and happiness. I have not travelled alone. So many have walked by my side, pushed me from behind, and led the way back when I veered off track. I have been inspired by the people who shared their stories on the path to healing. I am in awe of their courage, persistence, willingness to be vulnerable, and determination to succeed. I have held space, listened, heard, and recognized their pain, struggles, and eventual triumph. They are amazing.

Thanks to my husband, best friend, and number one fan and supporter, **Tom Coates**, for his willingness to listen to my excitement about integrating a new idea at 1 a.m.; his tolerance for all the times I "had to write"; his enthusiastic support for completing redoing my office so I could work in comfort; his offers of tea, dinner, or anything else I might possibly need; his warm and enveloping love (even when I'm cranky or distracted); his unwavering belief in me. He has nourished me, sustained me, encouraged me, and allowed me the room to flourish and grow. I love him beyond measure.

Thanks to my parents—words can't express my gratitude for their love and support throughout my life. To my **Dad, Donald Hallett**—thanks to him for always telling me, "You're a good writer" and "You should be a teacher." I've taken his advice and I'm so happy! That's a personal (as we say in our family, because it's a big accomplishment that warrants a handshake). To my **Mom, Sandra Hallett**—she never hesitated to read *one more* draft, article, paper, or newsletter. Thanks to her for always cheering me on and reminding me to do what I love. She taught me to be a strong, independent woman and to reach for the stars. She enhances my sparkle. I hope she's enjoying this surprise (it's the first time I haven't shared my work with her and the suspense has been killing me).

Thanks to my wonderful, talented, amazing daughter, **Sandra Hallett**—all I can say to her is, "Wow." She has already done so much in her life and the future is wide open. Her talks, snuggles, questions, and faith in me have kept me grounded and on my toes. I hope she sees how much she's taught me and my total respect and support for her amazing path.

Thanks to **Andrea, Diana, Kathy, Kelly, Jen, Julie, Maria Clara**—what would I do without their friendship? They are who I want to call with good news, and who I lean on when times are tough. They are true rock stars. It would take another book to list all the ways I appreciate them and have learned, grown, and benefitted from having them in my life. My heart overflows with love and gratitude for them.

Special thanks to Barb, Beth, Brendan, Cheri, Jennifer, Jolene, KB, Mark, Michelle, and Sophie for saying just the right things at just the right times. They have no idea how much I appreciate and value them. I've told them in person, but I want to publicly thank them here for their support, wisdom, and many wonderful laughs. They inspire me.

To the Morgan James Publishing team: Special thanks to David Hancock, CEO & Founder for believing in me and my message. To my Author Relations Manager, Margo Toulouse, thanks for making the process seamless and easy. Many more thanks to everyone else, but especially Jim Howard, Bethany Marshall, and Nickcole Watkins.

About the Author

Dr. Kristina Hallett is a psychologist, professor, coach, and shamanic practitioner. She provides coaching, training, supervision, and therapeutic and shamanic services to motivated, involved professionals who are looking to make significant changes in their life. Dr. Hallett specializes in helping mid-career, working parents get off the stress train and bring back happy in order to increase resilience and productivity. She is completely committed to living a life of joy, and recognizes that happiness is a choice—a choice that comes from digging deeply and learning to accept oneself fully as perfectly imperfect.

Dr. Hallett knows that living your best life starts with being your own best friend. Through the practices of mindfulness and meditation, and through awareness of the universal energetic connection between all living beings, she has brought about massive positive changes in her own life and helped her clients bring about massive positive changes in their own lives. Having manifested the perfect job for her, along with surprising gifts of abundance and ordinary moments of gratitude and appreciation, she is the embodiment of walking her talk.

Dr. Hallett received a bachelor's degree in biology and psychology from Wellesley College. She was awarded a master's degree and a doctorate in Clinical Psychology by the University of Massachusetts. She is a Board Certified and Licensed Clinical Psychologist. Dr. Hallett has trained in the tradition of the Q'ero shamans of Peru, through the guidance of the Four Winds Society, and with other talented shamanic practitioners. She is also a Board Certified and Licensed Clinical Psychologist. Her work integrates the evidence-based practice of psychology with the spirit-led wisdom of the indigenous healers of Peru, to provide a unique perspective on personal and community healing. With an understanding based on modern quantum physics and psychological theory and practice, and a heart open to the mysteries of life, she guides her clients into living lives full of joy and promise.

Whether dealing with relationship issues, the stress of trying to do it all and not feeling successful, or general dissatisfaction with life, her work has transformed hundreds of people. She has published across a wide variety of venues, from peer-reviewed psychological journals to her Huffington Post blog. She is dedicated to spreading her knowledge of transformation widely, so that as many people as possible may benefit and move into living lives of joy and fulfillment.

Website: drkristinahallett.org
Email: kristinamhallett@gmail.com
Facebook: www.facebook.com/OwnBestFriend8SimpleSteps
Instagram: www.instagram.com/wisdom_healing
LinkedIn: www.linkedin.com/in/kristina-hallett-phd-abpp-ab307021

Thank You

Thank you for reading. I'm thrilled you took this step towards living a fantastic, stress-less, rockin' life. If you're still questioning whether the EMPOWERS process is for you (or if you skipped to the end to see what happens), here's a checklist to help you out.

How you can know for sure it's time for a change:

- More than once you've thought to yourself *something is missing in my life.*
- You have too much to juggle and not enough time.
- Self-care is a great idea, but not practical in your life.
- You're tired. All the time.
- You wonder what your inner purpose is (or if you're the only one without one).
- Your middle name should be Stress.
- You try to fall asleep, but can't get off the merry-go-round of endless worries.
- Time is passing really quickly.
- You just want to be happy.

If you checked at least one of those items, it's time for a change. If you checked three to five items, it's past time. If you checked six or more, hooray! This is *your* time to make a change.

If you are committed to fully mastering the EMPOWERS process in your life and want assistance on your journey, you can get in touch with me here: https://drhallett.wufoo.com/forms/z27s0v9073anw1. I'd love to talk with you!

Free Video Class: I have a companion video series that goes with this book. You can sign up for it at https://drkristinahallett.org.

Song List of Celebration: Sign up with your email address at https://drkristinahallett.org and access the song list that inspired me to write this book for *you*.

Words to EMPOWER: Send me an email about your biggest fear (kristinamhallett@gmail.com) and I will send you a list of words to empower you every day.

Morgan James
Speakers Group

We connect Morgan James published
authors with live and online events
and audiences who will benefit
from their expertise.